GCSE AQA

Chemistry

Required Practicals

Fire up the Bunsen burner — it's time to get to grips with those tricky GCSE Chemistry Required Practicals...

Luckily, this booklet has everything you need! It has heaps of write-in activities to develop your analysis and evaluation skills for all eight Required Practicals. And there's plenty of exam-style practice too — you'll be an AQA practicals pro in no time.

To make sure you pick up every mark you can, we've included a mark-by-mark breakdown for every exam-style question. Plus, there are example answers for each task. You'll find those goodies in your **free** Online Edition — what a treat!

Unlock your Digital Extras

This booklet includes a **free Online Edition** including **full answers**. To access them, just scan the QR code below or go to **cgpbooks.co.uk/extras**, then enter this code!

0026 7382 9431 5114

By the way, this code only works for one person. If somebody else has used this book before you, they might have already claimed the code.

Course Booklet

Published by CGP

From original material by Richard Parsons

Editors: Emma Clayton, Katherine Faudemer, Paul Jordin, Hannah Lawson

Contributors: Paddy Gannon, Jamie Sinclair, Jack Turner, Louise Watkins

With thanks to Jamie Sinclair for the proofreading.
With thanks to Beth Linnane for the copyright research.

ISBN: 978 1 83774 186 1
Printed by Elanders Ltd, Newcastle upon Tyne.
Clipart from Corel®
Illustrations by: Sandy Gardner Artist, email sandy@sandygardner.co.uk

Text, design, layout and original illustrations © Coordination Group Publications Ltd (CGP) 2024. All rights reserved.

This booklet contains procedures for practical activities. The procedures are covered in outline only and are not intended to be followed in the lab. Safety when carrying out practical work is the responsibility of schools and colleges. A full risk assessment should always be undertaken. CGP cannot be held responsible for any type of loss, damage or injury resulting from the content of these activities.

Photocopying this book is not permitted, even if you have a CLA licence.
Extra copies are available from CGP with next day delivery • 0800 1712 712 • www.cgpbooks.co.uk

Contents

✓ Use the tick boxes to check off the pages you've completed.

Practical 1 — Making Salts

Background Knowledge 2
Practical 3
Evaluation 5
Exam-Style Questions 6

Practical 2 — Neutralisation

Background Knowledge 7
Practical 10
Results and Analysis 12
Conclusions and Evaluation 14
Exam-Style Questions 15

Practical 3 — Electrolysis

Background Knowledge 16
Practical 18
Results, Analysis and Conclusions 20
Exam-Style Questions 22

Practical 4 — Temperature Changes

Background Knowledge 23
Practical 24
Results, Analysis and Conclusions 26
Evaluation 28
Exam-Style Questions 29

Practical 5 — Rates of Reaction

Background Knowledge 30
Practical — Activity 1 32
Results and Analysis 33
Conclusions and Evaluation 34
Practical — Activity 2 36
Results and Analysis 37
Conclusions and Evaluation 38
Exam-Style Questions 39

Practical 6 — Chromatography

Background Knowledge 40
Practical 41
Results and Analysis 42
Conclusions and Evaluation 43
Exam-Style Questions 44

Practical 7 — Identifying Ions

Background Knowledge 45
Practical 46
Conclusions and Evaluation 49
Exam-Style Questions 51

Practical 8 — Water Purification

Background Knowledge 52
Practical — Activity 1 53
Analysis and Evaluation 54
Practical — Activity 2 55
Results, Analysis and Evaluation 57
Exam-Style Questions 58

Practical 1: Making Salts

Required Practical 1

Background Knowledge

In this practical, you'll be making **salt crystals** by reacting together an **acid** and a **base**.

Task 1 Circle the correct words in the definitions below.

> **ACID** — a substance that forms aqueous solutions with a pH of **less than / greater than** 7.
> **BASE** — a substance with a pH **less than / greater than** 7.
> **ALKALI** — a base that dissolves in water to form a solution with a pH **less than / greater than** 7.

Task 2 Fill in the **ions** that make up the following salts.

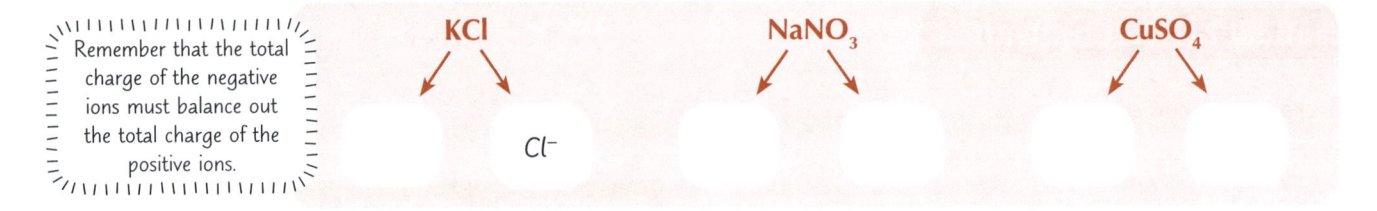

Remember that the total charge of the negative ions must balance out the total charge of the positive ions.

KCl → ☐ Cl^-

NaNO$_3$ → ☐ ☐

CuSO$_4$ → ☐ ☐

Task 3 Complete the equations for the following **neutralisation reactions**.

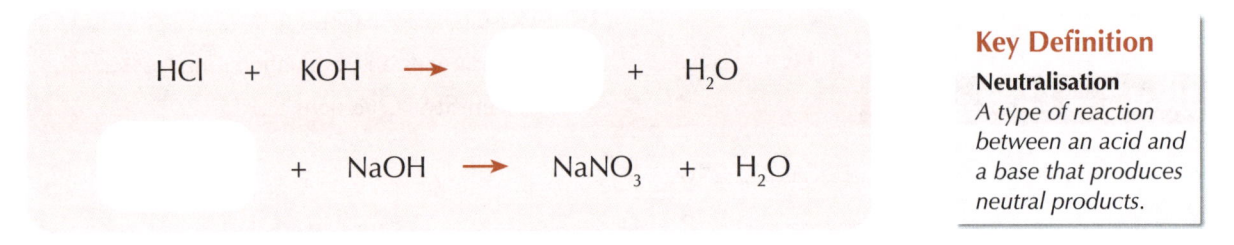

HCl + KOH → ☐ + H$_2$O

☐ + NaOH → NaNO$_3$ + H$_2$O

Key Definition
Neutralisation
A type of reaction between an acid and a base that produces neutral products.

Task 4 Jot down what you remember about **filtration** and **evaporation** to complete the mind maps. Think about what they are **used for** and what **equipment** is needed for each one.

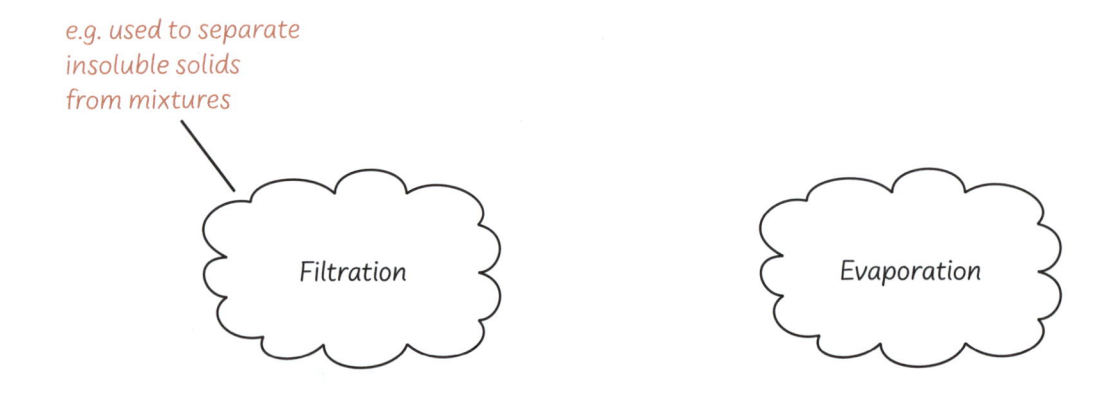

e.g. used to separate insoluble solids from mixtures — Filtration

Evaporation

Practical

Required Practical 1

Task 5 Use the **procedure** to help you answer the questions below.

Procedure

1. Set up a **Bunsen burner**, **tripod**, **gauze** and **heatproof mat** as shown in the diagram.
2. Add **40 cm³** of dilute **sulfuric acid** (**H₂SO₄**) to a **beaker**, and place it on the gauze.
3. Gently **heat** the acid. Turn off the Bunsen burner **just as** the acid starts to **boil**, and remove the beaker from the gauze.
4. Add a small amount of **copper(II) oxide** (**CuO**) powder to the acid. When stirred, the solution will turn **clear blue**.
5. **Repeat** step 4 until some copper(II) oxide **remains** after stirring.

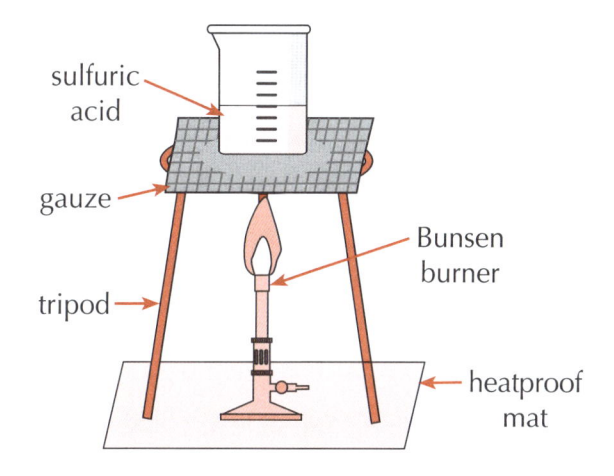

Why is copper(II) oxide powder added to the sulfuric acid in **excess**?

If something is added in 'excess', more of it is added than will react.

....

....

Write a **balanced symbol equation** for the reaction between the acid and base in this procedure. Include **state symbols**.

   +   ⟶   +

Task 6 Give three **safety precautions** that you should take when using the Bunsen burner to heat the acid in the procedure shown above.

1 ....
2 ....
3 ....

DISCUSS — **Neutralise the threat of poor practical technique...**
Why do you think dilute sulfuric acid is used in this procedure rather than concentrated sulfuric acid? Why is the acid removed from the heat just as it starts to boil? Discuss with a partner.

© CGP — not to be photocopied

Practical 1: Making Salts

Required Practical 1 — Practical

Task 7 **Draw** the filtration apparatus needed for the next step of the procedure. Label the **salt solution**, **excess base**, **filter paper**, **funnel** and **conical flask**.

Procedure

6. Set up the **filter paper** and **filter funnel** over a **conical flask**. **Filter** the contents of the beaker into the flask.

Task 8 Use the **crystallisation** procedure below to help you label the diagram.

Procedure

7. Pour the contents of the conical flask into an **evaporating basin** and use a **water bath** to gently evaporate the water from the salt solution.
8. When **crystals** start to form, turn off the heat and pour the contents of the evaporating basin into a **crystallising dish**. Leave it to crystallise for a day or two.
9. Take the crystals out of the dish pat them dry using filter paper.

Key Definition
Water bath
A container filled with heated water, used to heat substances more gently and evenly than direct heat.

Practical 1: Making Salts   © CGP — not to be photocopied

Evaluation

Required Practical 1

Task 9 The balanced equation for the reaction of **copper(II) oxide** with **hydrochloric acid** is:
2HCl + CuO → CuCl$_2$ + H$_2$O

Samiyah says that by using **hydrochloric acid** instead of sulfuric acid, but keeping the volume and concentration of the acid the same, you will only need to add **half** the amount of copper(II) oxide. Is Samiyah correct? Explain your answer.

You can use the equation you wrote in Task 5 to help you with this.

....
....
....
....

Task 10 **Hydrated** copper(II) sulfate forms bright **blue crystals**. **Anhydrous** copper(II) sulfate is a **white powder**. This practical may produce blue crystals, a white powder, or a combination of both.

Two students carry out the procedure to produce pure copper(II) sulfate. India produces a **white powder** whereas Keiran produces **blue crystals**. Suggest what India might have done differently to Keiran.

....
....

Key Definitions
Hydrated salt
A salt that has water molecules present in its crystal structure.
Anhydrous salt
A salt containing no water molecules.

Task 11 The **yield** of a reaction is the mass of product made. Explain how each of the following changes to the procedure shown in tasks 5-8 would affect the yield of the experiment.

A student repeats the experiment but adds **half** the volume of **sulfuric acid**.	The student then repeats the experiment with the full volume of sulfuric acid but **half** the mass of **copper(II) oxide**.

DISCUSS

Anhydrous grapes in cookies — sneaky little blighters...

An electric water bath sets and maintains a constant, specified temperature. Discuss the pros and cons of using an electric water bath instead of a Bunsen burner in this experiment. Would it affect the results?

Required Practical 1 — Exam-Style Questions

Task 12 Try these **exam-style** questions.

1   A student is trying to make pure calcium chloride crystals by reacting an acid with an insoluble metal carbonate. They suggest the following method:

1. Add 40 cm³ of dilute sulfuric acid to a beaker.
2. Use a Bunsen burner to heat the beaker until the acid is hot, then remove the beaker from the heat.
3. Add calcium carbonate powder to the beaker until some of it remains after stirring.
4. Pour the contents of the beaker into an evaporating basin and use a water bath to gently heat the salt solution until all the water has evaporated.

1.1 This method will not produce pure calcium chloride crystals.
Explain why, and suggest how the method can be improved.

....

....

....

....

....

....

....

[3]

1.2 Zinc chloride is an ionic compound containing Zn^{2+} ions. The student attempts to make zinc chloride crystals by adding an excess of insoluble zinc carbonate to hydrochloric acid. Complete the balanced symbol equation for this reaction.

.....HCl + ... → $ZnCl_2$ + H_2O + ...

[2]

1.3 When the reaction is complete, some zinc carbonate will remain after stirring.
Suggest another way that the student will know when the reaction is complete.

....

....

[1]

1.4 Sodium carbonate is soluble in water.
Another student suggests that to make sodium chloride, they could add sodium carbonate to hydrochloric acid, then filter out the excess base and evaporate off the water.
Explain why this suggestion will not produce a pure sample of sodium chloride.

....

....

[1]

[Total 8 marks]

Practical 1: Making Salts

Practical 2: Neutralisation

Background Knowledge

Required Practical 2

Ever received a solution of sodium hydroxide for Christmas and wondered what its concentration might be? Me neither. But if that did happen, you could work it out for yourself using a **titration**.

Task 1 Dylan has a sample of a **strong alkali**. He adds some **universal indicator** to the alkali, then slowly adds a **strong acid** until the acid is in excess. Fill in the table to describe the **pH** and **colour** of the solution at the different points during Dylan's experiment. Use the options in the box.

< 7   red   green   > 7   purple   7

	pH	Colour
At the start of the experiment		
When the solution is neutral		
At the end of the experiment		

Key Definition
Excess
More than is needed for the reaction to go to completion.

Task 2 Complete the **mind map** below about **pH indicators**.

Think about why you might choose to use something other than an indicator.

- **What are they?**
- **Uses**
- **pH indicators**
- **Limitations / Alternatives**
- **Examples**

Task 3 Fill in the gaps to complete the sentences below.

When an acid reacts with a base, a _____ and _____ are formed.

This is called a _____ reaction. The products of the reaction

have a pH of ____ — in other words, they're _____.

Required Practical 2

Background Knowledge

Task 4 **Circle** the ion that all acids form in water. **Underline** the ion that all alkalis form in water.

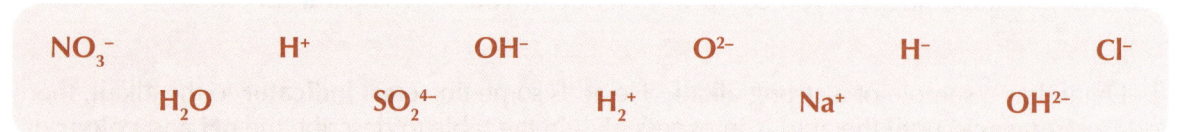

NO_3^- H^+ OH^- O^{2-} H^- Cl^-
H_2O SO_2^{4-} H_2^+ Na^+ OH^{2-}

Write a half equation for the reaction of these two ions in solution. Include state symbols.

....

Task 5 A scientist burns some **propane** (C_3H_8) in oxygen. The equation for the reaction that occurs is shown on the right.

$C_3H_8 + 5O_2 \rightarrow 4H_2O + 3CO_2$

Write down the **simplest ratio** of moles of propane burned to moles of carbon dioxide formed.

C_3H_8 : CO_2
　　　:

The reaction produced **9 moles** of **carbon dioxide**.

How many moles of **propane** reacted?	How many moles of **oxygen** reacted?	How many moles of **water** were produced?
.... moles	.... moles	.... moles

Task 6 Use the **relative atomic masses** from the table to answer the following questions.

What is the relative formula mass of **Mg(OH)$_2$**?

M_r = ...

A compound has the formula **X$_2$SO$_4$**. Its relative formula mass is 142. What is the **identity** of element X?

Element = ...

Element	A_r
B	11
C	12
Cl	35.5
H	1
K	39
Li	7
Mg	24
Na	23
O	16
S	32

DISCUSS — **My favourite base is at the bottom of a cheesecake...**
Mira has a beaker of dilute hydrochloric acid. She plans to use litmus paper to measure the acidity of the solution. Discuss with a partner whether this will work. What could she use instead?

Practical 2: Neutralisation   © CGP — not to be photocopied

Background Knowledge

Required Practical 2

Task 7 Lucille is making some **salt solutions** by dissolving different amounts of sodium chloride, NaCl, in different volumes of water.

Complete the table below to show the **concentrations** of the solutions she has made. Which two solutions have the same concentration?

To convert from cm^3 to dm^3, divide by 1000.

Solution	Amount of salt dissolved (g)	Volume of water	Concentration (g/dm^3)
A	150	2.0 dm^3	75
B	90	1.5 dm^3	
C	38	0.95 dm^3	
D	140	500 cm^3	
E	51	680 cm^3	
F	72	240 cm^3	

Solution .... and solution .... have the same concentration.

Lucille wants to know the concentration of solution **A** in **mol/dm³**.

Calculate the M_r of NaCl. A_r(Na) = 23, A_r(Cl) = 35.5

M_r = ...

Use your M_r value to calculate the concentration of solution **A** in mol/dm³.
Give your answer to three significant figures.

To convert from grams to moles, divide by the M_r.

.... mol/dm³

Task 8 Sachin has 350 cm³ of 2.5 mol/dm³ potassium carbonate (K_2CO_3) solution.

Calculate the **mass** of potassium carbonate that is dissolved in this solution.
Give your answer to two significant figures. A_r(K) = 39, A_r(C) = 12, A_r(O) = 16

.... g

Practical 2: Neutralisation

Practical

Required Practical 2

Task 9 A method for determining how much acid is required to neutralise a sample of dilute alkali is shown below. This method is called a **titration**. Use the words in the box along with the definitions on the right to fill in the blanks in the method.

> end-point   indicator   pipette filler   tap   burette

Procedure

1. Use a pipette and _____ to draw up a set volume of alkali and transfer it to a conical flask.
2. Add two or three drops of indicator to the flask. The indicator should be a single indicator with a sharp colour change, e.g. phenolphthalein.
3. Making sure the tap is closed, fill a _____ with acid and record its initial volume.
4. Do a rough titration: Place the flask of alkali under the burette and open the _____ on the burette to add the acid to the alkali, giving the flask a regular swirl.
5. Stop adding the acid when the _____ changes colour. Record the volume of acid left in the burette.
6. Repeat the titration, but this time add the acid to the alkali a little bit at a time. Go especially slowly near the _____.
7. Calculate the volume of acid added, then repeat the titration until you get two results within 0.10 cm³ of each other.

Key Definitions

Pipette
A glass tube used to measure out an accurate volume of liquid.

Pipette Filler
A piece of apparatus used to draw up liquid into a pipette.

Burette
A long glass tube used for measuring liquids. It has a tap at the bottom that the liquid can be released through. The scale measures from top to bottom.

End-point
The point during a titration when all the acid/alkali has been neutralised.

Task 10 A diagram of the equipment used in **Task 9** is shown below. **Label** the diagram using the words from the box. You won't need to use of all the words.

> beaker
> mass balance
> pipette
> test tube
> conical flask
> thermometer
> tap
> burette
> measuring cylinder
> gas syringe

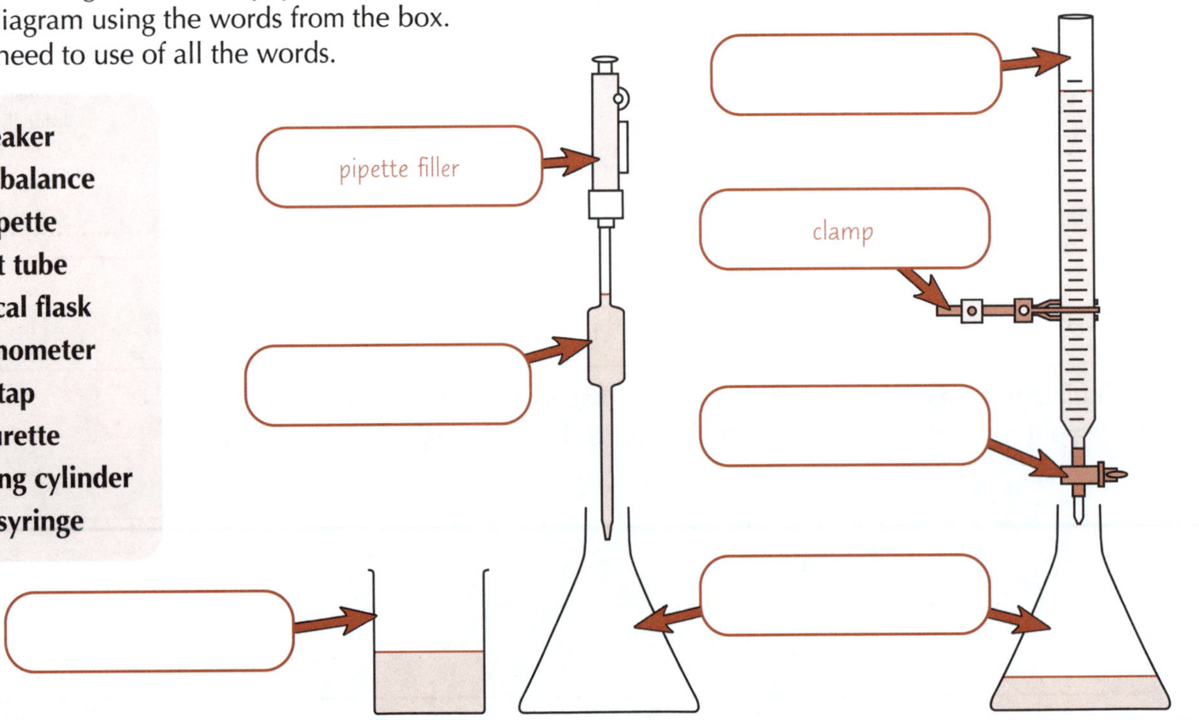

(Labels shown: pipette filler, clamp)

Practical 2: Neutralisation

Practical

Required Practical 2

Task 11 A student is using a **pipette** to measure out some alkali for a titration.

She starts by rinsing the pipette with some of the alkali. Explain why this is a good idea.

....

....

Put the following sentences in order to show **how** she should use the pipette to measure out the alkali.

        Use the wheel to drop the level down to the line.

        Place the bottom of the pipette into a beaker of alkali.

        Push the button to dispense the alkali.

1   Attach a pipette filler to the top of the pipette.

        Hold the pipette over an empty conical flask.

        Scroll the wheel slowly on the pipette filler to draw the alkali up to about 3 cm above the line.

Pipette Filler

You might use a different type of pipette filler, e.g. one with a rubber bulb. They all work in the same way — they create a vacuum to draw the liquid upwards, and then release the vacuum to push the liquid out again.

Task 12 Give three **safety precautions** you should take when filling a burette with acid or alkali.

1. ....

2. ....

3. ....

Task 13 Tick **two** boxes to show how **volume measurements** should be taken from a burette.

☐ From the middle of the meniscus   ☐ From eye-level

☐ From the top of the meniscus   ☐ From above

☐ From the bottom of the meniscus   ☐ From below

Key Definition
Meniscus
The curved upper surface of a liquid.

DISCUSS — **I've got a silicon carbide lab coat — it's burette-proof...**

Look at the procedure in **Task 9**. Why do you think it is important to do a rough titration first? What problems might you run into if you didn't? Discuss your thoughts with a partner.

© CGP — not to be photocopied   Practical 2: Neutralisation

Required Practical 2: Results and Analysis

Task 14 Amelia carries out a titration experiment. Her results are shown below. During the experiment, **dilute sulfuric acid** was added to 25 cm³ of 0.25 mol/dm³ **sodium hydroxide solution**. Complete the table by calculating the **volume of acid** added in each titration.

	Initial reading on burette (cm³)	Final reading on burette (cm³)	Volume of acid added (cm³)
Rough titration	0.00	19.60	19.60
First titration	19.60	38.60	
Second titration	0.00	18.85	
Third titration	18.85	38.10	
Fourth titration	0.00	18.90	

Task 15 One of the titrations in the table above produced an **anomalous** result. **Circle** the correct option in the sentence below and **explain** why it doesn't fit with the rest of the data.

Key Definition
Anomalous Result
A result that doesn't fit with the rest of the data.

The **first / second / third / fourth** titration had an anomalous result.

....
....
....

Task 16 Calculate the **mean volume** of sulfuric acid that was required to neutralise 25 cm³ of 0.25 mol/dm³ sodium hydroxide solution. Give your answer in dm³.

You should ignore any anomalous or rough titration results when calculating the mean.

.... dm³

Practical 2: Neutralisation

Results and Analysis

Required Practical 2

Task 17 Amelia attempts to calculate the number of **moles** of NaOH that reacted to two significant figures. Her calculation is shown below.

moles = concentration × volume = 0.25 × 25 = <u>6.3 moles</u> (2 significant figures)

Explain what Amelia did wrong and calculate the **correct** number of moles of NaOH to two significant figures.

.... moles

Task 18 The equation for the reaction is: $2NaOH_{(aq)} + H_2SO_{4(aq)} \rightarrow Na_2SO_{4(aq)} + 2H_2O_{(l)}$

Explain how you can use this equation to work out the number of moles of **sulfuric acid** that reacted.

....

....

....

Calculate the **concentration** of the sulfuric acid in **mol/dm³**. Give your answer to two significant figures.

You should use your unrounded answers from earlier calculations here.

.... mol/dm³

Task 19 Calculate the concentration of the sulfuric acid in **g/dm³**. Give your answer to two significant figures. $A_r(H) = 1$, $A_r(S) = 32$, $A_r(O) = 16$

You should use your <u>unrounded</u> concentration in mol/dm³ for this calculation.

.... g/dm³

Concentrate your efforts on finishing this practical...

DISCUSS Look at the table of results in **Task 14**. Discuss with a partner how you think these results might be different if Amelia had used 25 cm³ of **0.50 mol/dm³** sodium hydroxide solution instead.

© CGP — not to be photocopied

Practical 2: Neutralisation

Required Practical 2

Conclusions and Evaluation

Task 20 Why do you think it's **important** to do the following during a titration? What **problems** might you encounter if you didn't? Write some notes.

| Repeat the titration until you get two results that are within 0.10 cm³ of each other. | Calculate the mean of your results. |

Task 21 Look at your answers to **Task 14**. Calculate the range of the results.

range = ... cm³

Ignore any rough or anomalous results when calculating things like range, uncertainty and the mean.

Use the range to calculate the **uncertainty** of the **mean** in cm³.
Give your answer in the form **mean ± uncertainty**.

Uncertainty = range ÷ 2
            =

.... ± .... cm³

Key Definitions
Range
How spread out a set of data is.
Uncertainty
The amount of error a result might have.

Task 22 Amelia used **phenolphthalein** as the indicator in her experiment. Explain why this is **more suitable** for a titration than **universal indicator**.

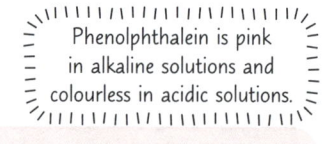

Phenolphthalein is pink in alkaline solutions and colourless in acidic solutions.

....
....
....

Task 23 Amelia plans to carry out the titration again. Give one **modification** she could make to her experiment that would help her to see the colour change more **clearly**.

....
....

Practical 2: Neutralisation © CGP — not to be photocopied

Exam-Style Questions

Required Practical 2

Task 24 Try these **exam-style** questions.

1   A student is carrying out a titration to determine the concentration of a dilute solution of potassium hydroxide, KOH.

1.1 The student has a pipette with a volume of 50 cm^3. Explain why the student **cannot** use this pipette to measure out 25 cm^3 of the potassium hydroxide solution.

....

....
[1]

1.2 The student fills a burette with 0.10 mol/dm^3 hydrochloric acid and places a beaker underneath. The student then briefly opens the tap on the burette and lets some of the acid out. Suggest why the student does this.

....

....
[1]

The student removes the beaker and replaces it with a conical flask containing 25 cm^3 of the potassium hydroxide solution and a few drops of litmus (an indicator). The student then carries out the titration.

1.3 Litmus is red in acidic solutions and blue in alkaline solutions.
     Describe what the student will observe at the end-point of the titration.

....

....
[1]

1.4 Give one advantage of using a burette to dispense the acid, rather than a measuring cylinder.

....

....
[1]

1.5 It takes 17.64 cm^3 of hydrochloric acid to neutralise the potassium hydroxide solution.
     Calculate the concentration of the potassium hydroxide solution in mol/dm^3.
     Give your answer to two significant figures.
     The equation for the reaction is: HCl + KOH → KCl + H$_2$O.

.... mol/dm^3
[4]

[Total 8 marks]

Practical 2: Neutralisation

Practical 3: Electrolysis

Required Practical 3

Background Knowledge

In this practical, we'll investigate what happens when two different **aqueous solutions** are **electrolysed**.

Task 1 Add the metals in the box to the **reactivity series**, listing them in order from **most** reactive at the top to **least** reactive at the bottom.

Reactivity Series

....
....
Carbon
....
....
Hydrogen
....
....

Hint: the metals that are less reactive than hydrogen are ones you might find in jewellery.

Magnesium   Zinc
    Sodium
            Silver
Iron   Copper

Task 2 **Draw lines** to match the words to their definitions.

Oxidation   Reduction   Cation   Anion

Positive ion   Gain of electrons   Negative ion   Loss of electrons

Task 3 **Ionic equations** show only the particles that **react** and the products they form.

For the following ionic equation, circle the reactant that is being **reduced**.

$$Mg + Cu^{2+} \rightarrow Mg^{2+} + Cu$$

Explain how you know this.

Practical 3: Electrolysis

© CGP — not to be photocopied

Background Knowledge

Required Practical 3

Task 4 For each of the following **half equations**, decide whether they would take place at the **anode** (positive electrode) or **cathode** (negative electrode) during electrolysis.

	Anode	Cathode
$Al^{3+} + 3e^- \rightarrow Al$	☐	☐
$2H^+ + 2e^- \rightarrow H_2$	☐	☐
$2O^{2-} \rightarrow O_2 + 4e^-$	☐	☐
$2Br^- \rightarrow Br_2 + 2e^-$	☐	☐

Key Definitions

Half equation
An equation showing either the reduction or oxidation part of a redox reaction, in terms of the movement of electrons.

Redox reaction
A reaction that involves the transfer of electrons.

Task 5 **Electrolysis** can be performed on **molten ionic compounds** and **aqueous solutions**. Give all the **ions** present in the following:

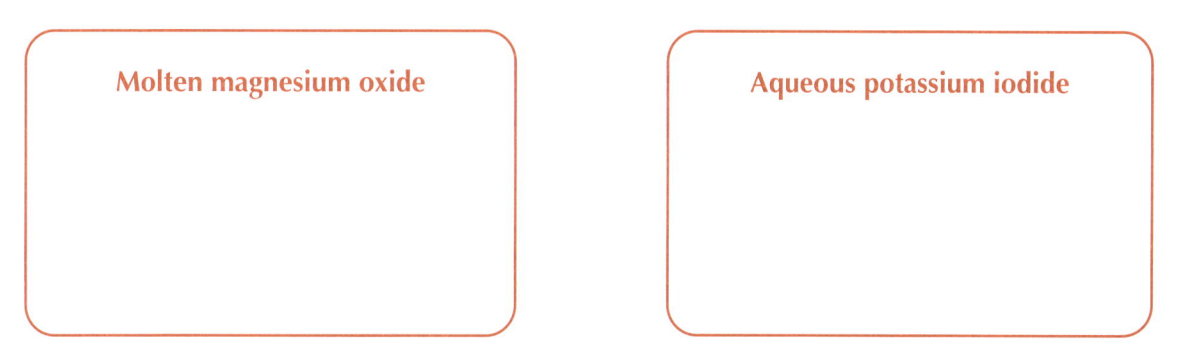

Molten magnesium oxide

Aqueous potassium iodide

Task 6 Fill in the gaps in the flow chart to show what **products** are made at each electrode during the electrolysis of an **aqueous solution** of a **metal salt**.

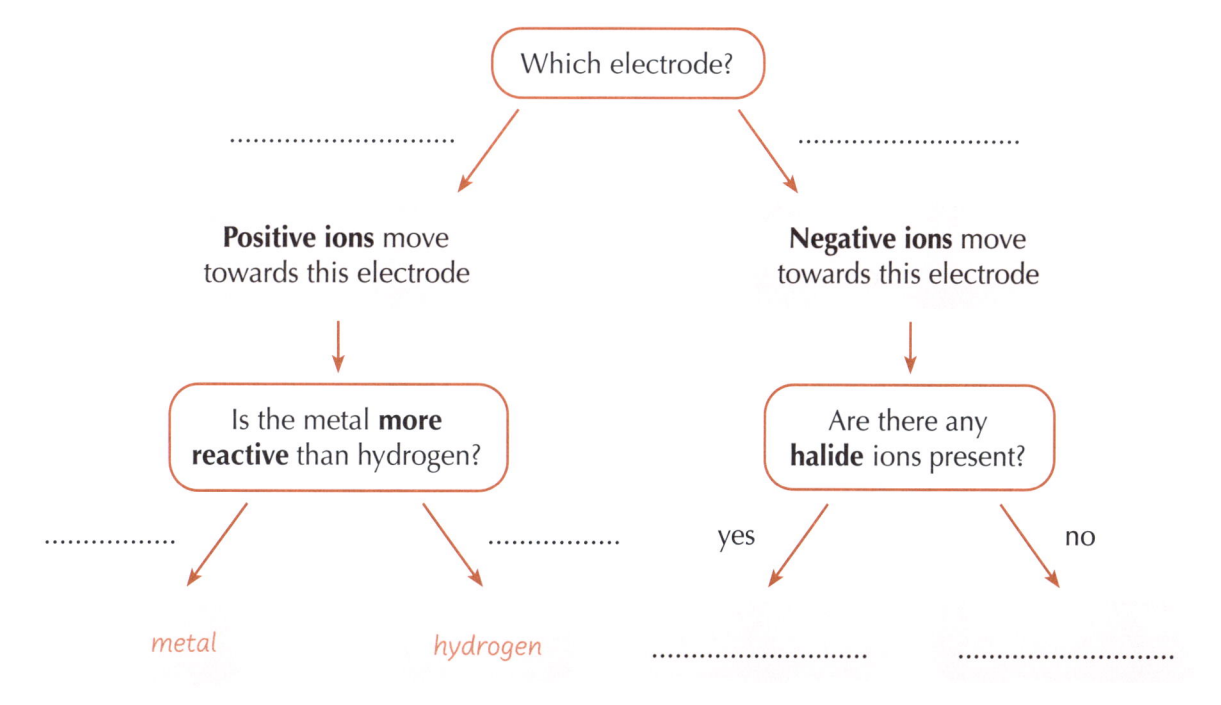

Which electrode?

.... → **Positive ions** move towards this electrode → Is the metal **more reactive** than hydrogen? → .... metal / .... hydrogen

.... → **Negative ions** move towards this electrode → Are there any **halide** ions present? → yes .... / no ....

DISCUSS — **Never trust iodide — I can't tell you all the times halide...**
You need to be able to write half equations for the reactions that happen at the electrodes. Are there any patterns that you can use to work out unknown half equations? Discuss with a partner.

Practical 3: Electrolysis

Required Practical 3

Practical

Task 7 In this practical, we'll be electrolysing **copper(II) chloride** solution and **sodium chloride** solution. Write a **hypothesis** for what you expect to be produced at each electrode when these solutions are electrolysed.

You'll need to give the states as well as the names of the products.

Copper(II) chloride solution

.... will be produced at the anode.

.... will be produced at the cathode.

Sodium chloride solution

Key Definition
Hypothesis
A statement of what you expect to happen in an experiment — it can be accepted or rejected.

Task 8 The procedure for setting up an **electrochemical cell** is given below. Draw a diagram of the set up, labelling the **electrolyte solution**, **anode** and **cathode**.

Procedure

1. Pour the **electrolyte solution** into a **beaker**.
2. Add a **lid**, e.g. a piece of cardboard with two holes in it. Poke the **electrodes** through the holes.
3. Use crocodile leads to connect the electrodes to a **low-voltage power supply**.
4. **Turn on** the power supply.
5. **Observe** and **record** what happens at each electrode.

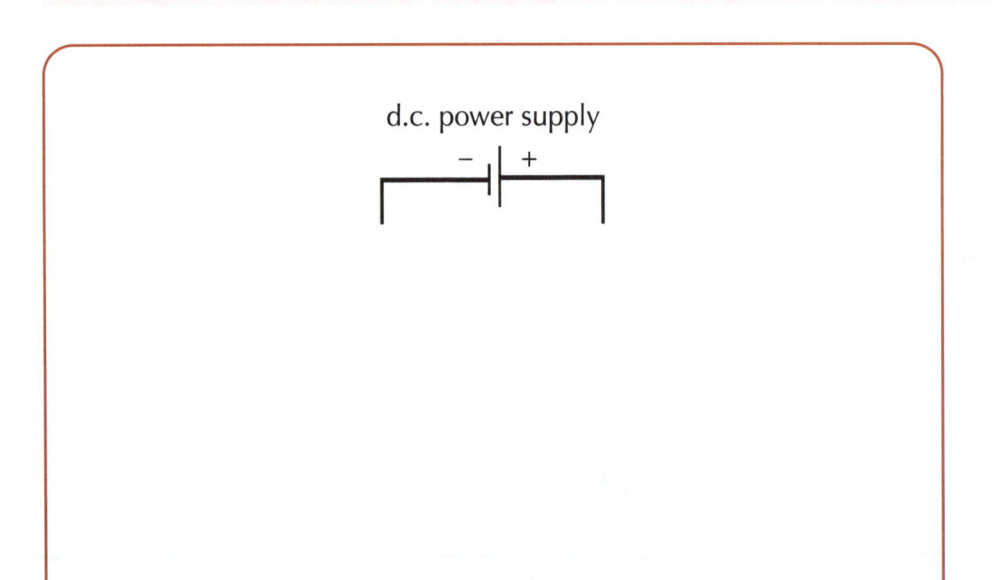

d.c. power supply

Key Definitions
Electrolyte
A liquid or solution that can conduct electricity.

Electrode
A solid that conducts electricity and is submerged in the electrolyte.

Practical 3: Electrolysis

Practical

Required Practical 3

Task 9 You can use inert **carbon rods** as electrodes in this practical.

Why is it important that the electrodes are **inert**?

....

You must make sure that the electrodes **aren't touching** when you set up your electrochemical cell. Suggest why.

....

....

Why should you **rinse** your electrodes and beaker with **distilled water** between solutions?

....

....

Task 10 For each of the following elements, suggest what you would **observe** if it was formed during electrolysis, and how you could **test** for its presence. Think about the **state** you would expect to find the element in.

Chlorine

Hydrogen

Oxygen

DISCUSS — Mitochondria are the powerhouses... Sorry, wrong cell...

Different halogens have different states at room temperature. Discuss with a partner what you would expect to observe if fluorine, bromine or iodine were produced at an electrode.

© CGP — not to be photocopied

Practical 3: Electrolysis

Results, Analysis and Conclusions

Required Practical 3

Task 11 The table below shows some **example results** from this practical.
For each observation, state which **element** was produced.

Solution	Anode (positive electrode)		Cathode (negative electrode)	
	Observations	Element produced	Observations	Element produced
Copper(II) chloride	Bubbles Turns damp litmus paper white		Red/brown coating on electrode	
Sodium chloride	Bubbles Turns damp litmus paper white		Rapid bubbles	

Task 12 Do the example results in the table above line up with your hypotheses from **Task 7**? Circle whether your hypotheses would be **accepted** or **rejected** and explain why.

Copper(II) chloride solution	Sodium chloride solution
Anode: I **accept** / **reject** my hypothesis. Explanation: I hypothesised that .... would be produced at the anode. .... was produced.	**Anode:** I **accept** / **reject** my hypothesis. Explanation:
Cathode: I **accept** / **reject** my hypothesis. Explanation:	**Cathode:** I **accept** / **reject** my hypothesis. Explanation:

DISCUSS — **I accept / reject my hypothesis that chemistry is boring...**
Testing hypotheses is the backbone of how science works. Discuss what you think makes a good hypothesis. Can you think of anything else you'd like to find out based on your results from this practical?

Results, Analysis and Conclusions

Required Practical 3

Task 13 Write the balanced **half equations** for the reactions that occurred at each electrode.

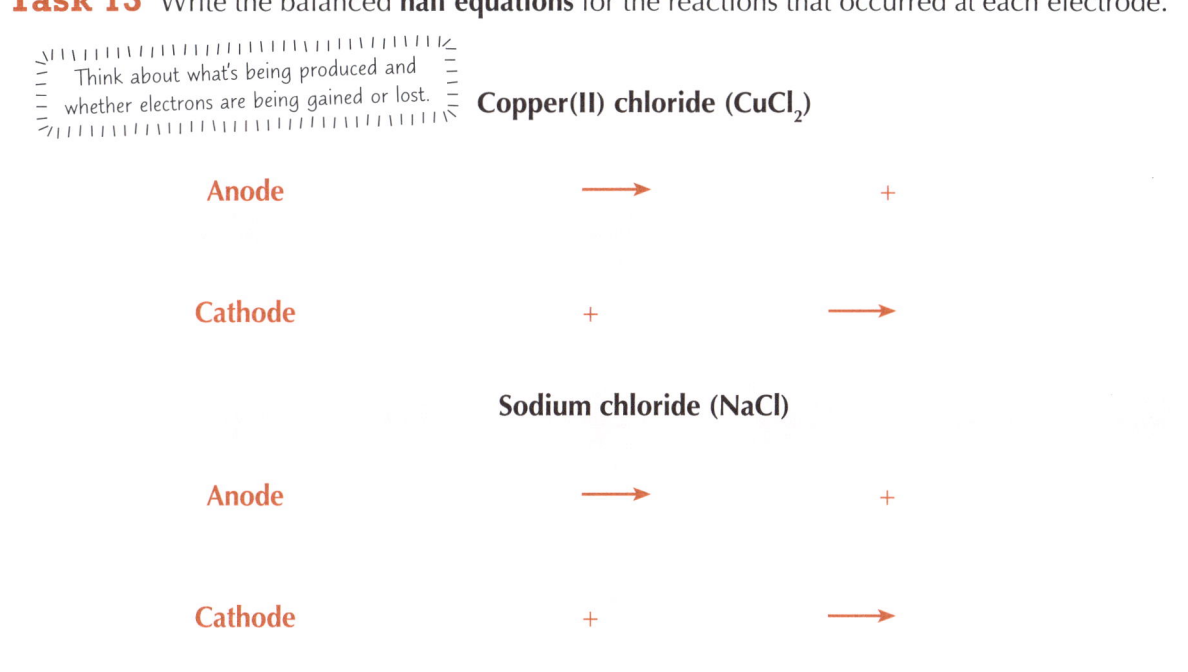

Think about what's being produced and whether electrons are being gained or lost.

Copper(II) chloride (CuCl$_2$)

Anode   →   +

Cathode   +   →

Sodium chloride (NaCl)

Anode   →   +

Cathode   +   →

Task 14 A student electrolysed **copper(II) sulfate solution**, weighing the cathode every five minutes. The graph below shows the change in mass of the cathode over time.

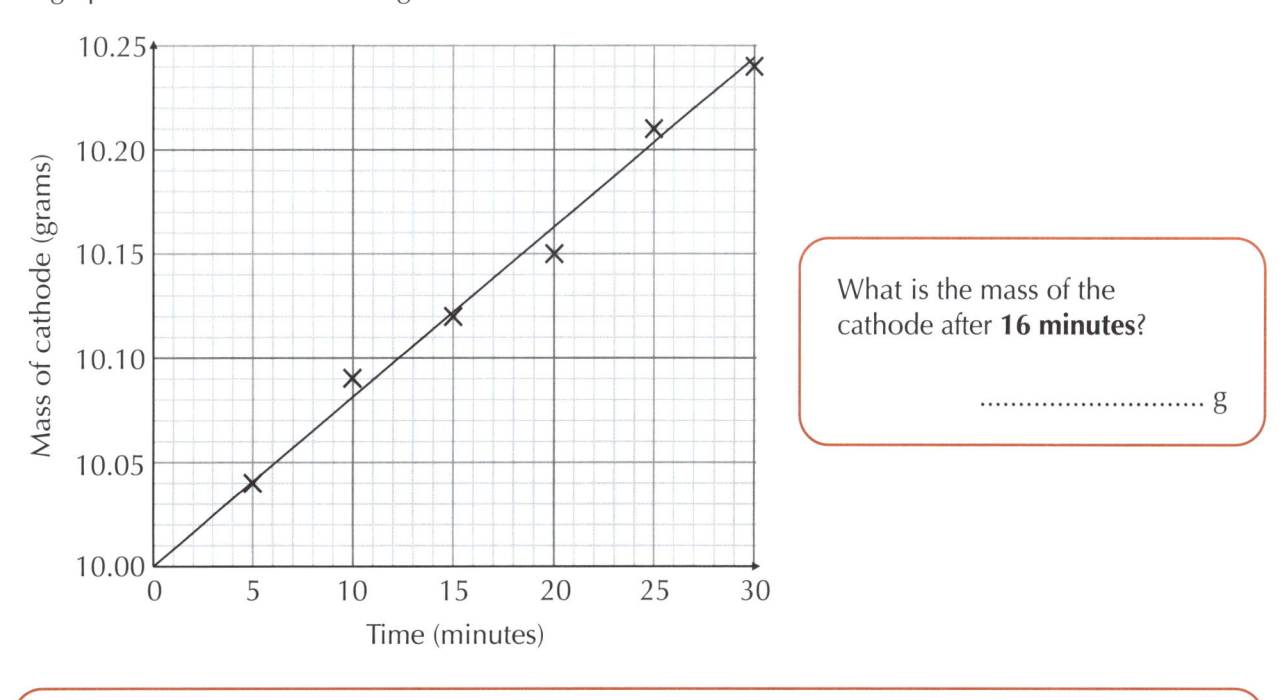

What is the mass of the cathode after **16 minutes**?

.... g

Describe and explain how the mass of the cathode **changed** over time.

....
....
....

© CGP — not to be photocopied

Practical 3: Electrolysis

Required Practical 3

Exam-Style Questions

Task 15 Try these **exam-style** questions.

1   Some students investigated the electrolysis of aqueous silver nitrate solution.
    Silver nitrate solution contains Ag⁺ and NO₃⁻ ions.
    The diagram below shows the apparatus the students used.

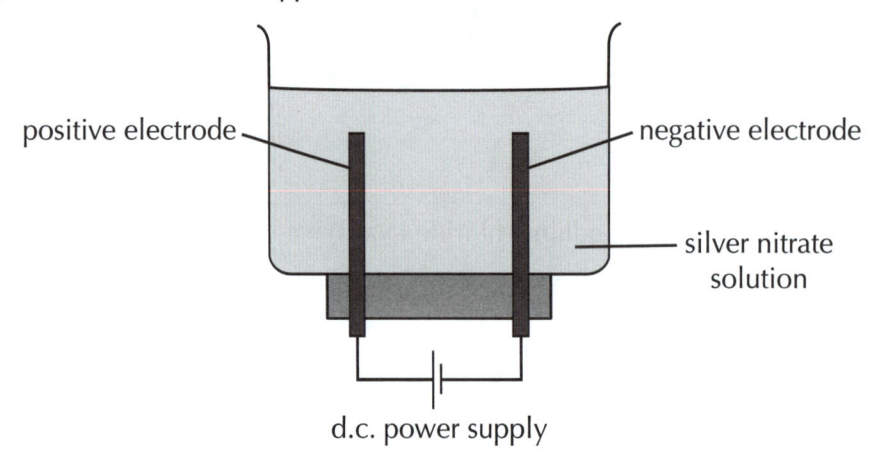

After five minutes, a coating of silver could be seen on the negative electrode.

1.1 Explain why silver ions move towards the negative electrode.

....
[1]

1.2 Complete the balanced half equation for the reaction at the negative electrode.

.... + ... → Ag

[1]

1.3 A gas is produced at the positive electrode. Name the gas and describe how it is formed.

....

....
[2]

1.4 Complete the balanced half equation for the reaction at the positive electrode.

4OH⁻ → .... + ... + ...

[1]

1.5 The students want to find out how the volume of gas produced changes over time.
     Outline how they could investigate this.

....

....

....

....
[4]

[Total 9 marks]

Practical 3: Electrolysis

Practical 4: Temperature Changes

Background Knowledge

Required Practical 4

In this practical we're investigating **temperature changes**. Most reactions involve some sort of change in temperature, so there are lots of ways to study how different **variables** affect temperature change.

Task 1 The heat energy in some chemical reactions is transferred from the reaction mixture to the surroundings. Suggest **two** ways to **reduce** this energy transfer when you are conducting an experiment.

....
....
....

Task 2 **Lines of best fit** can be drawn as straight lines or smooth curves.
Two copies of the same graph are shown below, with part of a line of best fit added.

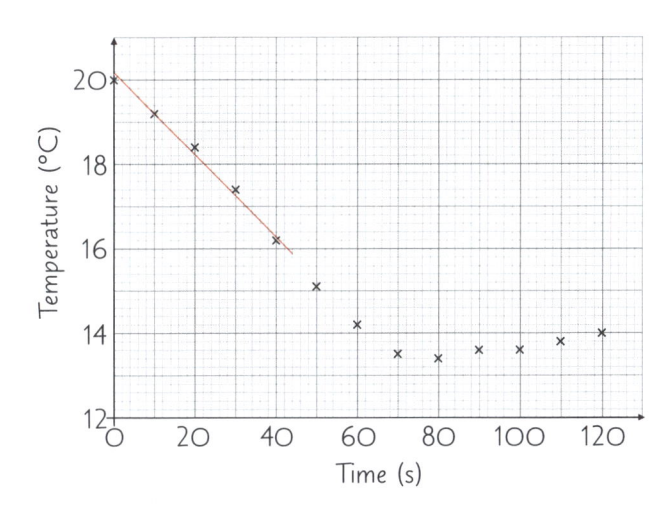

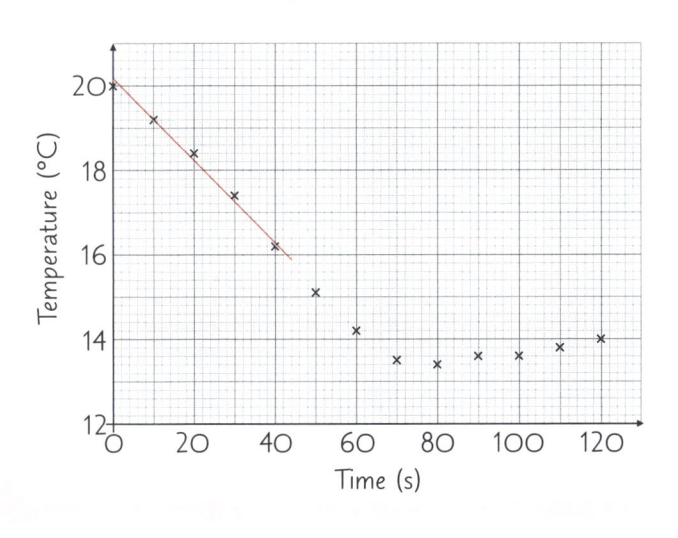

1. Use the line of best fit to estimate the temperature at a time of **38 seconds**. Give your answer to 3 significant figures.

   .... °C

2. On the first graph, extend the straight line of best fit and add a second straight line through the rest of the data points.

   ### Key Definition
   Line of best fit
   A straight line or curve on a scatter graph, drawn through or close to as many points as possible.

3. On the second graph, extend the existing line of best fit to make a smooth curve that passes as close as possible to the data points.

4. Use your curved line of best fit to estimate when the **minimum temperature** was reached. Give your answer to the nearest second.

   .... seconds

Lines of best fit can be curved or straight. Always check if the instructions for a task or question specify one or the other, and make sure you draw the right sort.

Hope that's got you warmed up...

DISCUSS With a partner, see if you can think of any reactions that result in a change in temperature. Do any of them have anything in common? What would you need to accurately measure the temperature?

| Required Practical 4 | **Practical** |

Task 3 The reaction between hydrochloric acid and sodium hydroxide solution results in an **increase** in temperature. An experiment to investigate how changing the **volume** of sodium hydroxide solution affects the **temperature change** in this reaction is outlined below.

Procedure

Add 30 cm³ of dilute hydrochloric acid to a polystyrene cup, then measure the temperature of the acid.

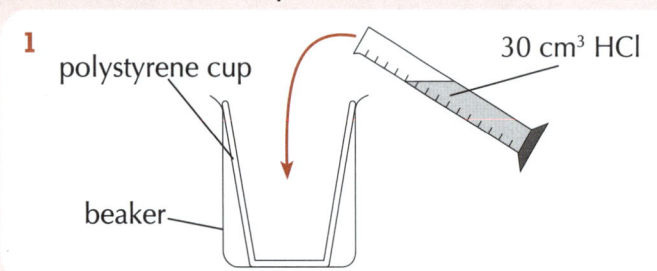

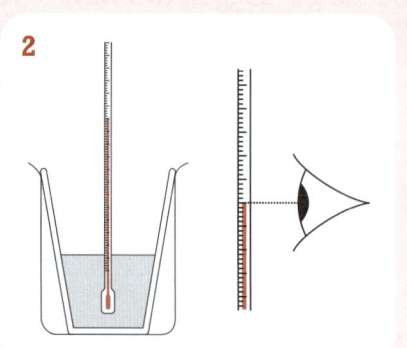

1. polystyrene cup, 30 cm³ HCl, beaker
2.

Add 5 cm³ of dilute sodium hydroxide solution to the acid, then quickly fit a lid to the cup. Use the thermometer to stir the mixture. Record the highest temperature the mixture reaches.

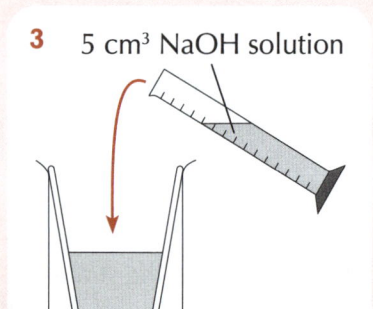

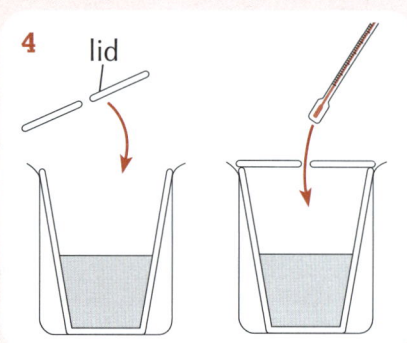

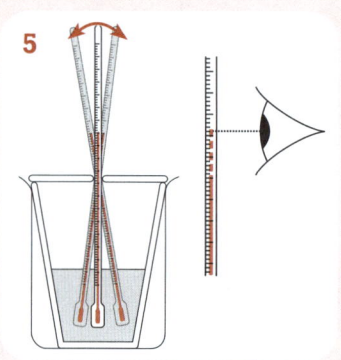

3. 5 cm³ NaOH solution
4. lid
5.

Carry on adding sodium hydroxide solution, 5 cm³ at a time. Record the maximum temperature reached each time. Keep going until you've added a total of 40 cm³ of sodium hydroxide solution.

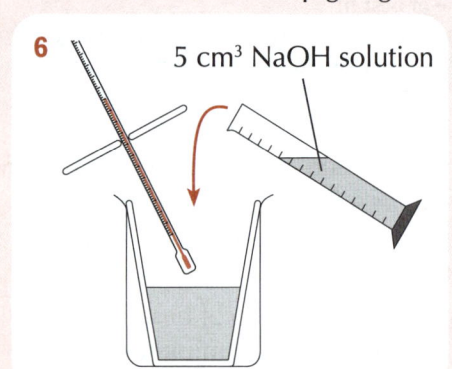

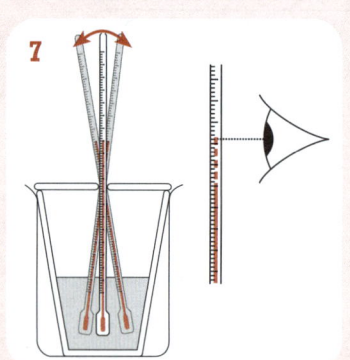

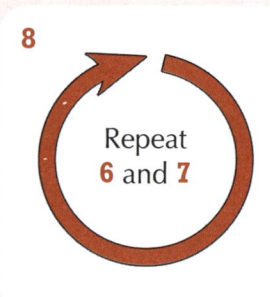

6. 5 cm³ NaOH solution
7.
8. Repeat **6** and **7**

Both reactants in this experiment are **corrosive**. What **safety precautions** should you take when working with the corrosive chemicals used here?

....

....

....

Practical 4: Temperature Changes © CGP — not to be photocopied

Practical

Required Practical 4

Task 4 **Neutralisation reactions** between acids and alkalis release energy which heats the surroundings. Add more **variables** to the mind map that could affect the **temperature change** in a neutralisation reaction.

Key Definition
Neutralisation
A reaction between an acid and a base that produces neutral products.

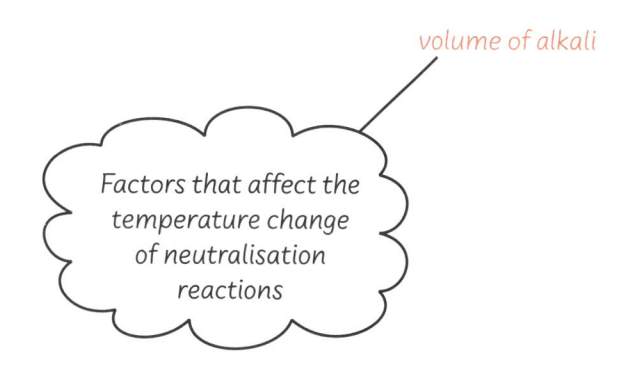

volume of alkali

Factors that affect the temperature change of neutralisation reactions

Task 5 Two more reactions which result in an increase in temperature are given below. For each one, briefly **describe** how you could **adapt** the procedure given in **Task 3** to carry out the given investigation.

Acid Plus Carbonate

Hydrochloric acid reacts with copper carbonate: $2HCl_{(aq)} + CuCO_{3(s)} \rightarrow CuCl_{2(aq)} + CO_{2(g)} + H_2O_{(l)}$
Investigate how changing the **mass** of **copper carbonate** affects the temperature change in this reaction.

Acid Plus Metal

Sulfuric acid reacts with magnesium: $H_2SO_{4(aq)} + Mg_{(s)} \rightarrow MgSO_{4(aq)} + H_{2(g)}$
Investigate how changing the **concentration** of the **acid** affects the temperature change in this reaction.

DISCUSS **Keep a lid on it...** except when you have to take the lid off to add more reactant...
All the reactions covered on these pages involve an increase in temperature. Discuss whether you would need to change the method for a reaction where the temperature decreased instead. Why, or why not?

Results, Analysis and Conclusions

Required Practical 4

Task 6 Keira carried out the experiment described in Task 3. Her **results** are shown below. **Complete** the table by working out the **mean value** for the maximum temperature reached for each volume of sodium hydroxide solution.
Give your answers to **3 significant figures**. The first one has been done for you.

Volume of NaOH solution added (cm³)	Maximum temperature (°C) — Trial 1	Maximum temperature (°C) — Trial 2	Mean maximum temperature (°C)
0	19.8	20.5	20.2
5	23.5	23.9	
10	26.0	25.8	
15	28.8	28.2	
20	31.0	30.5	
25	32.1	32.4	
30	32.3	32.4	
35	32.1	31.5	
40	30.5	31.0	

Task 7 Using the data from the table above, plot a graph on this grid to show the relationship between the volume of NaOH solution and temperature.
Use the **mean temperature values** you calculated and choose a **sensible scale** for each axis.

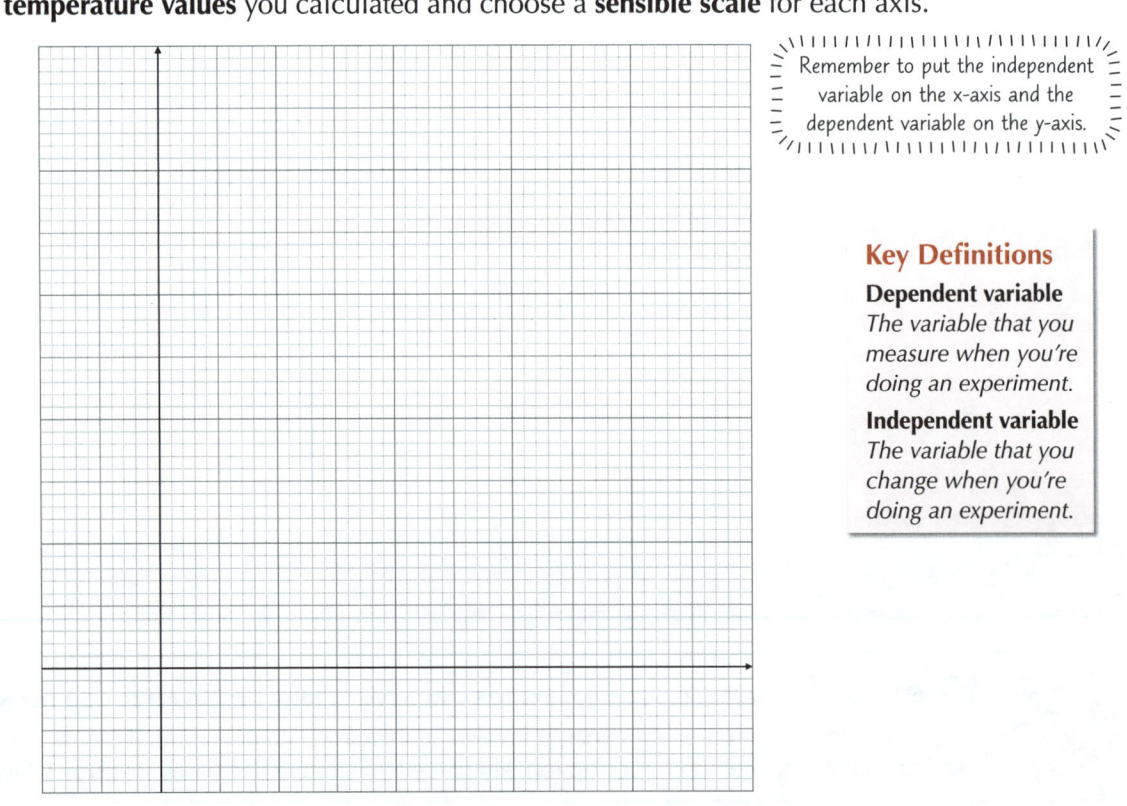

Remember to put the independent variable on the x-axis and the dependent variable on the y-axis.

Key Definitions
Dependent variable
The variable that you measure when you're doing an experiment.

Independent variable
The variable that you change when you're doing an experiment.

Practical 4: Temperature Changes

Results, Analysis and Conclusions

Required Practical 4

Task 8 Noah carried out **his own version** of the experiment. The graph below shows Noah's data.

Draw two **straight lines of best fit** on Noah's graph, extending them so that they cross.

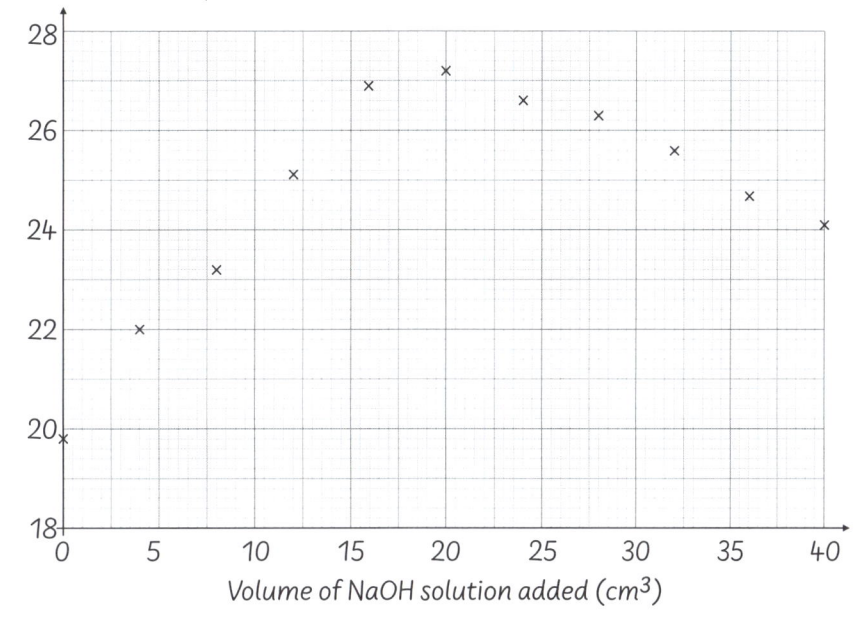

Mean maximum temperature (°C) vs *Volume of NaOH solution added (cm³)*

Task 9 The maximum temperature reached in this reaction can be **estimated** using the lines of best fit.

Calculate the temperature change that occurred in this reaction.

.... °C

The maximum temperature is reached at the point where enough sodium hydroxide has been added to **completely neutralise** the acid.

Estimate the volume of sodium hydroxide needed to completely neutralise the acid used in Noah's experiment: ....cm³

Task 10 There were some **differences** between Noah's method and Keira's. For example, Noah used the **same reactants** as Keira but in **different concentrations**.

Using information from Keira's table and Noah's graph, give **one other way** in which Noah's method was different from Keira's.

....

....

On special occasions, I wear my suit of best fit...

DISCUSS With a partner, compare the results shown for Keira's and Noah's experiments. In which experiment do you think the reactants were in a higher concentration? Why do you think that? Can you tell for sure?

Practical 4: Temperature Changes

Required Practical 4

Evaluation

Task 11 The procedure given in Task 3 will **not** always give an **accurate** value for the temperature change in the reaction.

Looking in particular at the method used in **steps 6-8** of the procedure, suggest one reason why the true temperature change is likely to be **higher** than the values recorded in this experiment.

....

....

Explain how this might affect the **reproducibility** of the results.

Key Definition
Reproducibility
How easy it is for different people to get similar results when carrying out the same experiment.

....

....

....

....

Suggest **two changes** to this experiment that would improve the **accuracy** of the data recorded.

1	2

Task 12 When a line of best fit is **extended** and used to estimate values outside the range of the data points, this is called **extrapolation**.

Hint: think about what the graph would look like if you only had the first few data values for one of the experiments in this practical.

Explain, using temperature change investigations as an example, why you might get **misleading** estimates if you extrapolate beyond the range of your data.

....

....

....

....

....

DISCUSS

For reproducible results, stick 'em in the photocopier...

Are there any other steps in this method that might affect the accuracy of your results, apart from any you've mentioned above? Discuss with a partner any other potential sources of error in this experiment.

Exam-Style Questions

Required Practical 4

Task 13 Try these exam-style questions.

1. Copper can be displaced from a solution of copper chloride by adding a more reactive metal. For example, the reaction between copper chloride and zinc is:

    $$CuCl_{2(aq)} + Zn_{(s)} \rightarrow ZnCl_{2(aq)} + Cu_{(s)}$$

    This type of reaction is exothermic. A student is designing an investigation into how the temperature change is affected by changing which metal is added.

1.1 The metals that the student is considering comparing are sodium, calcium, magnesium, zinc, iron and tin. Using your knowledge of the reactivity of metals, suggest why using sodium and calcium would not give a fair comparison with the other metals on this list.

    ....

    ....
    [1]

    The experiment will involve a series of tests. In each test, the student will add a sample of a different metal to a test tube containing copper chloride solution. The same volume and concentration of copper chloride solution will be used in each test.

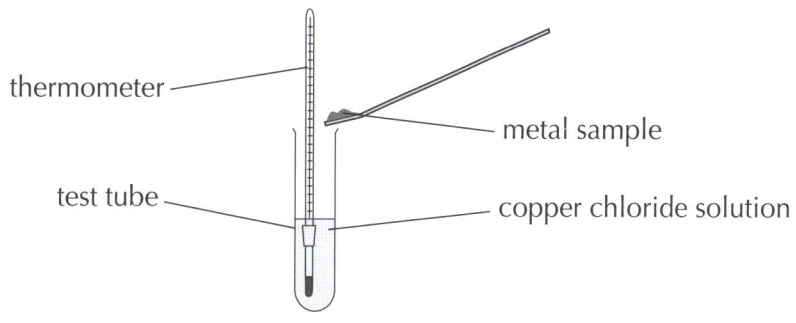

1.2 Which reactant should be in excess in each test, the metal or the copper chloride solution? Explain your answer.

    ....

    ....

    ....
    [2]

1.3 The student says, "In each test, I will record the temperature of the reaction mixture every 15 seconds for 2 minutes." Explain how this part of the method could be improved.

    ....

    ....

    ....
    [2]

    [Total 5 marks]

Practical 5: Rates of Reaction

Required Practical 5

Background Knowledge

Here we'll be investigating how changes in **concentration** affect the **rates of reactions**. You'll be treated to two experiments — one involving **measuring gases** and the other looking at **turbidity** changes. Yippee.

Task 1 The graph below shows the **rate** of a reaction taking place under three **different conditions**.

The y axis could also show the amount of reactant used.

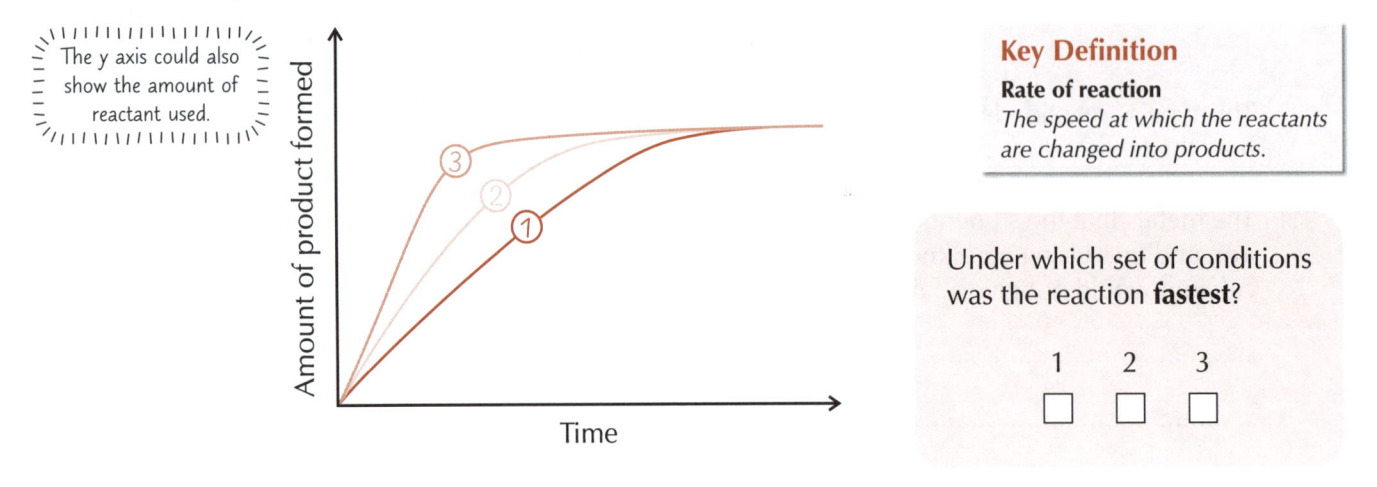

Key Definition
Rate of reaction
The speed at which the reactants are changed into products.

Under which set of conditions was the reaction **fastest**?

1 ☐   2 ☐   3 ☐

Task 2 Make notes on the factors that influence the rate of a reaction. Think about **how** and **why** they affect the rate, referring to **collision theory** and whether the **state** of the reactants matters. You may find it helpful to include **diagrams** in your notes. The first one has been done for you.

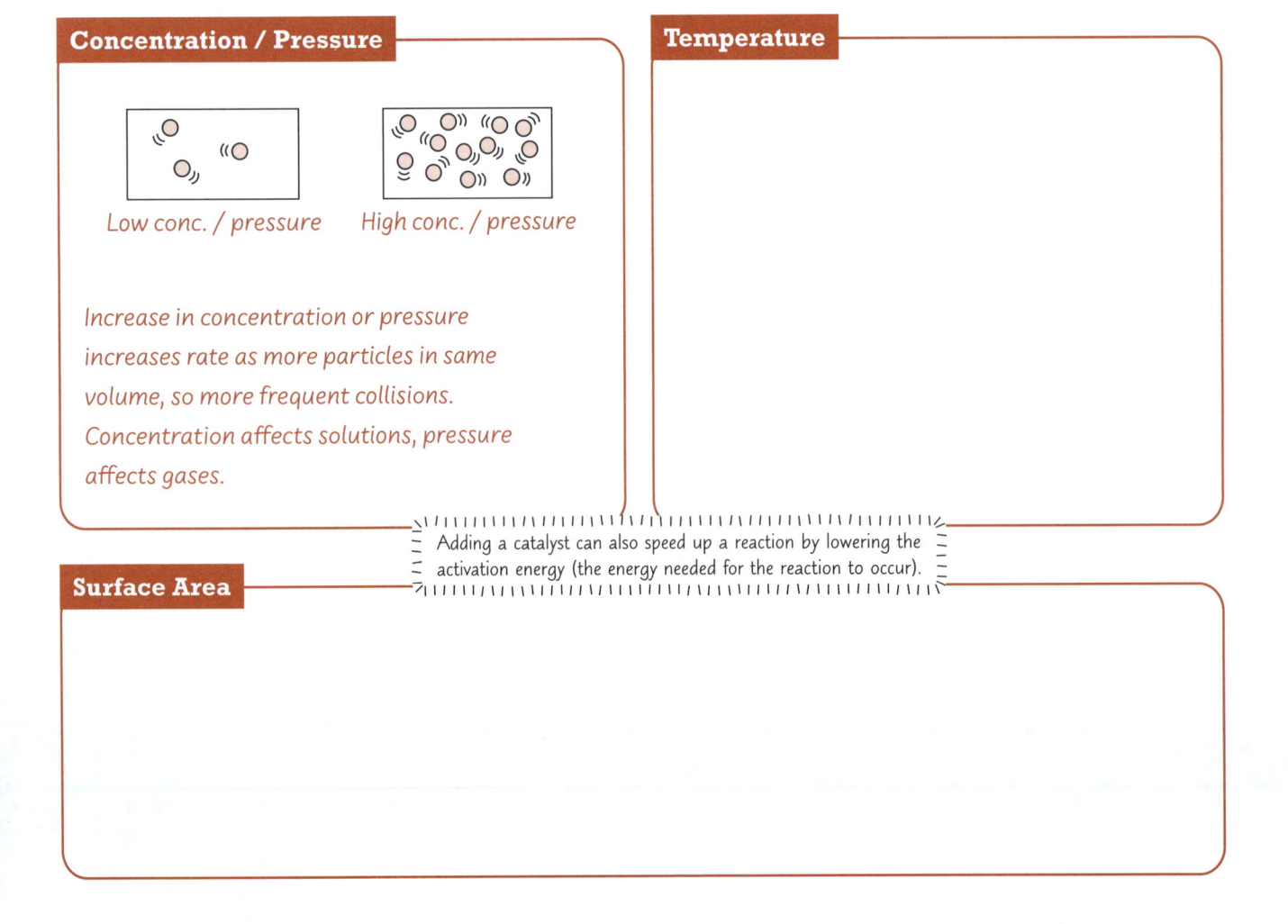

Concentration / Pressure

Low conc. / pressure   High conc. / pressure

Increase in concentration or pressure increases rate as more particles in same volume, so more frequent collisions. Concentration affects solutions, pressure affects gases.

Temperature

Adding a catalyst can also speed up a reaction by lowering the activation energy (the energy needed for the reaction to occur).

Surface Area

Background Knowledge

Required Practical 5

Task 3 Draw **lines of best fit** on the graphs below.
They should be **smooth curves** that come close to all the points.

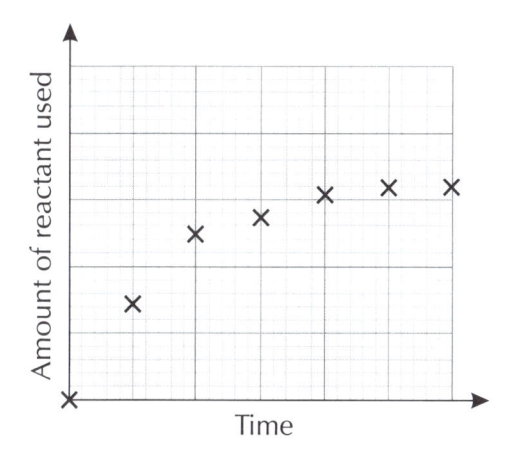

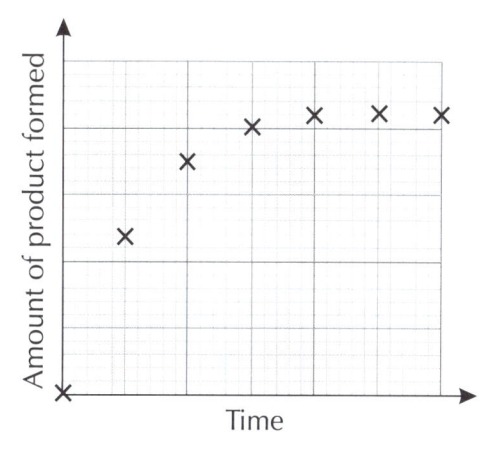

Task 4 The graph below shows the **volume of gas** released by a reaction over **time**.

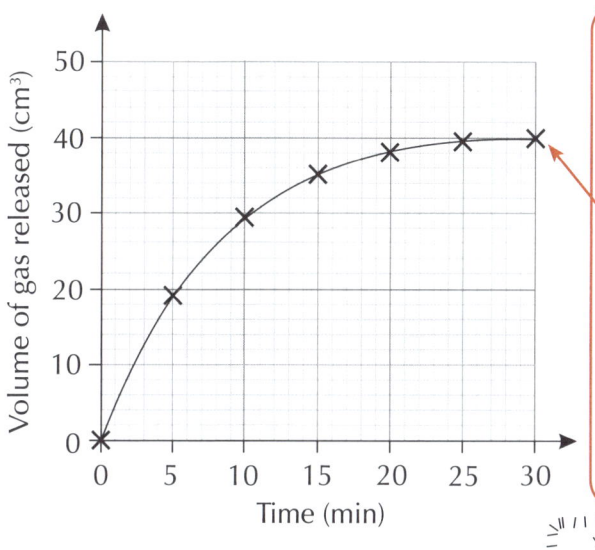

Complete this calculation to find the **mean** rate of the reaction during the time shown on the graph. Give your answer to **2 significant figures**.

$$\text{Rate of reaction} = \frac{\text{Amount of product formed}}{\text{Time}}$$

The total amount of gas released (product formed) was .... cm³.

The time taken was .... minutes.

Mean rate of reaction = ... ÷ .... = ...

.... cm³/min

You can also find the rate using the amount of reactant used instead of the amount of product formed, depending on what you measure in your experiment.

What is the rate of the reaction at **10 minutes**?
Give your answer to **2 significant figures**.

1. Draw a tangent on the graph
2. Find the coordinates of two points on the tangent
3. Use the formula below to calculate the gradient:
   gradient = change in y ÷ change in x

Key Definition

Tangent
A straight line that touches a curve at a point without crossing it.

.... cm³/min

I'm working at a mean rate of 4.6 p/h (puns per hour)...

Think about some real life chemical reactions, e.g. combustion (burning), rusting, photosynthesis (how plants make glucose). Discuss whether they are fast or slow, and why you think that is.

© CGP — not to be photocopied

Practical 5: Rates of Reaction

| Required Practical 5 | # Practical — Activity 1 |

Task 5 This activity involves measuring the rate of reaction between **magnesium** and **hydrochloric acid**. The **concentration** of the acid will be changed, but all other variables will stay the same.

A hypothesis is a statement of what you expect to happen in an experiment — it can be accepted or rejected.

Write a **hypothesis** stating how you expect the **concentration** of hydrochloric acid to affect the **rate** of this reaction.

Use **collision theory** to explain your hypothesis.

Task 6 Use the **procedure** to answer the question below.

Key Definition
Delivery tube
A thin glass tube used to allow gas to travel from one container to another.

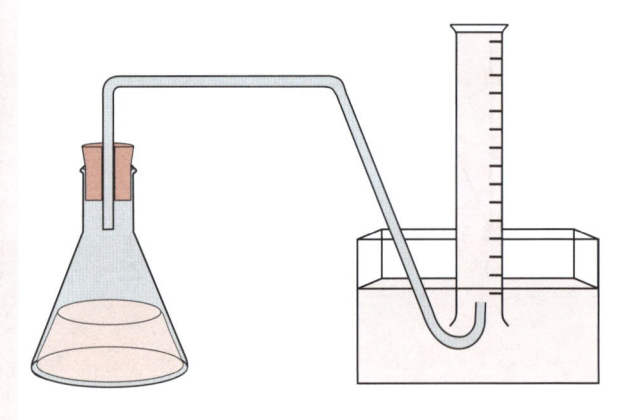

Procedure

1. Add **50 cm³** of **1.0 mol/dm³** hydrochloric acid to a **conical flask**.
2. Set up the **conical flask** with a **bung**, **delivery tube**, **water trough** and **measuring cylinder** as shown in the diagram. Make sure the upturned measuring cylinder is **completely filled** with water.
3. Remove the bung from the flask and add a **3 cm** strip of **magnesium ribbon** to the acid.
4. Quickly put the bung back on the flask and start a **stopwatch**.
5. Every **10 seconds**, check the measuring cylinder and record the **volume** of hydrogen gas. Continue until the volume **stops increasing**.
6. Now **repeat** the experiment using the same volume of **1.5 mol/dm³** hydrochloric acid.

Measurements of the volume of gas produced must be taken **every 10 seconds**.
Describe how you can work with your partner to ensure the measurements are made **accurately**.

....
....
....
....

Practical 5: Rates of Reaction

Results and Analysis

Required Practical 5

Task 7 The table below shows some **example results** from this experiment. **Plot** both sets of data on the graph paper below and draw a **line of best fit** for each. **Label** each line with the acid concentration.

Time (seconds)		10	20	30	40	50	60	70	80	90
Volume of gas produced (cm^3)	1.0 mol/dm^3	7.0	15.0	20.0	29.0	34.0	41.0	45.0	49.0	49.0
	1.5 mol/dm^3	11.0	21.0	33.0	43.0	50.0	54.0	55.0	55.0	55.0

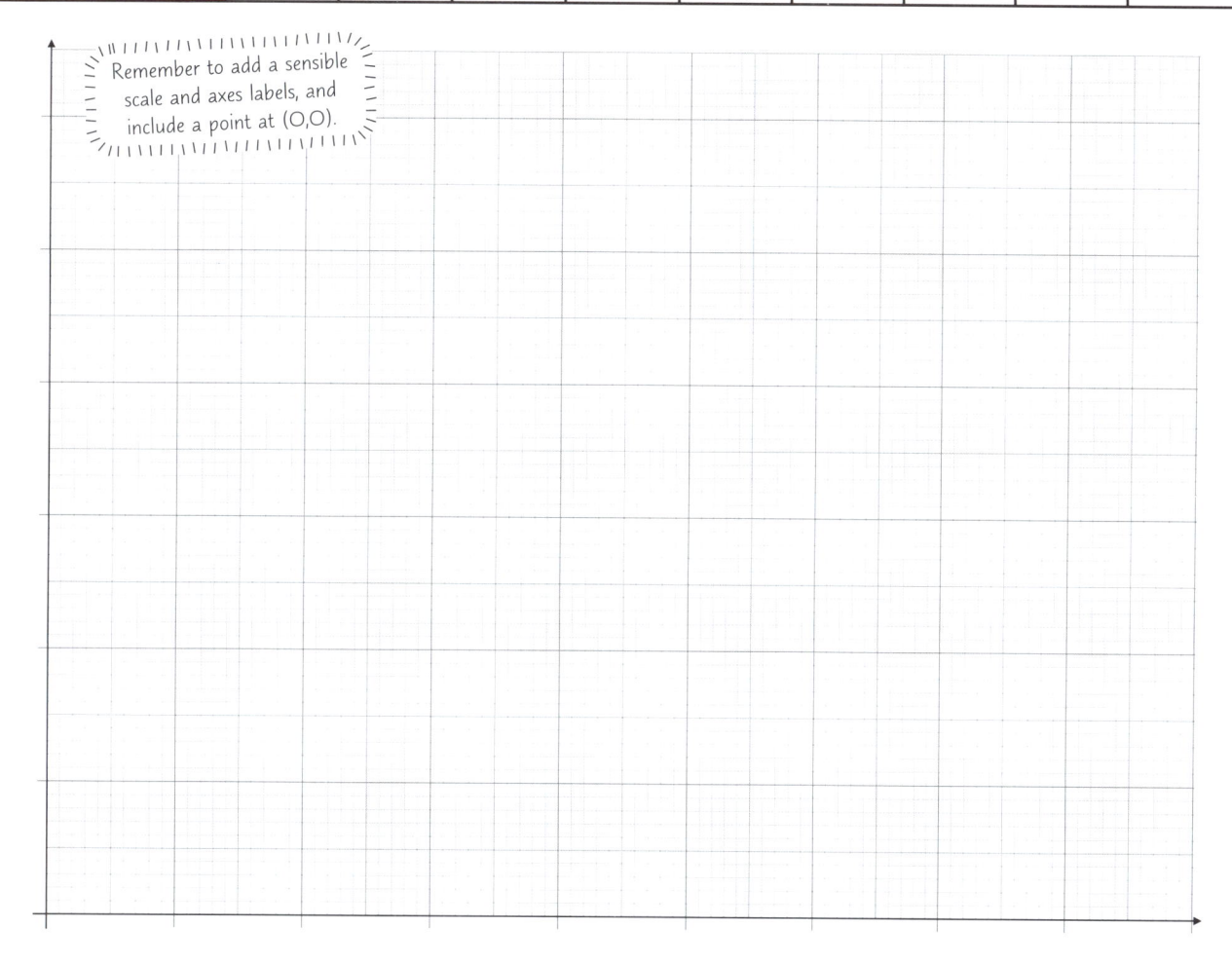

Remember to add a sensible scale and axes labels, and include a point at (0,0).

Task 8 Based on the example results, state whether you would accept or reject your hypothesis from **Task 5**. Use the **graph** to explain your answer.

DISCUSS — **Higher concentration of beans = more gas production...**
What products are formed in this reaction? Discuss with a partner, using your knowledge of how metals react with acids. You can even have a go at writing a balanced symbol equation.

© CGP — not to be photocopied

Practical 5: Rates of Reaction

Required Practical 5

Conclusions and Evaluation

Task 9 Calculate the **mean rate** of reaction until the reaction **finished** (when no more gas was produced) for both concentrations of acid. Give your answers to **two significant figures**.

There's a formula for this on page 31.

1.0 mol/dm³:

.... cm³/s

1.5 mol/dm³:

.... cm³/s

Task 10 Calculate the rate of reaction at **60 seconds** for both concentrations of acid. Draw a **tangent** on the graph for each concentration and find the **gradient** of the lines. Give your answers to **two significant figures**.

1.0 mol/dm³:

.... cm³/s

1.5 mol/dm³:

.... cm³/s

Task 11 How do the rates you calculated in **Task 9** compare to the rates you calculated in **Task 10**? Use **collision theory** to explain why they're different.

....
....
....
....
....
....

Practical 5: Rates of Reaction

Conclusions and Evaluation

Required Practical 5

Task 12 A student repeats the experiment but uses a **gas syringe** instead of a water trough and measuring cylinder, as shown in the diagram below.

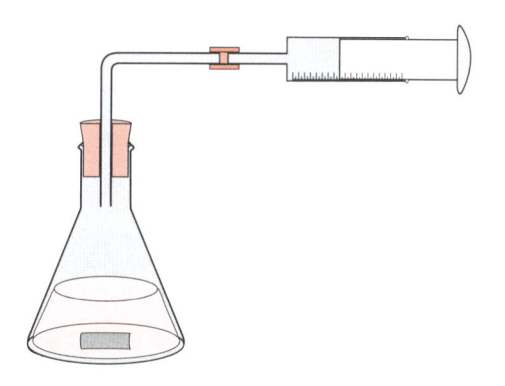

Key Definition
Gas syringe
A syringe used to insert, withdraw or measure gas.

The student tests **three** different concentrations of hydrochloric acid: **1.0 mol/dm³**, **1.5 mol/dm³** and **2.0 mol/dm³**.

Give one **advantage** of using a gas syringe instead of a water trough and measuring cylinder.

....

....

How would you expect the rate of reaction with **2.0 mol/dm³** hydrochloric acid to compare to the rate with **1.5 mol/dm³** hydrochloric acid?

....

The student measures a **larger overall volume** of gas when using **1.5 mol/dm³** hydrochloric acid compared to **1.0 mol/dm³**. Explain why.

....

....

....

The student **does not** measure a larger overall volume of gas when using **2.0 mol/dm³** hydrochloric acid compared to **1.5 mol/dm³**. Suggest why.

....

The student says that using the same mass of **powdered** magnesium would **increase** the rate of the reaction. Are they correct? Explain your answer.

....

....

....

DISCUSS **If it's a gas syringe, how do you pick it up...?**
Discuss what you'd expect to see if you measured the mass of the open conical flask and its contents instead of collecting the gas. How would the change in mass compare to the volume of gas produced?

Practical 5: Rates of Reaction

Required Practical 5

Practical — Activity 2

Task 13 This next activity involves observing changes in the **turbidity** (cloudiness) of a solution. Fill in the missing **volumes** in the table below.

Procedure

1. Add 50 cm³ of 40 g/dm³ **sodium thiosulfate** solution to a **conical flask**.
2. Put the conical flask on a **piece of paper** with a **black cross** printed on it.
3. Add **10 cm³** of dilute **hydrochloric acid** to the conical flask while gently swirling the flask. Start a **stopwatch**.
4. Look down at the cross through the flask. When you can no longer see the cross, **stop** the stopwatch and **record** the time taken for the cross to disappear.
5. **Repeat** steps 1-4 another four times. For each repeat, mix the **original 40 g/dm³ solution** with **water** in different proportions, as shown in the table below. This will give a different **concentration** of sodium thiosulfate solution each time. The **total volume** of solution used, including the water, should be **the same** for each repeat.

Volume of sodium thiosulfate (cm³)	Volume of water (cm³)	Concentration of sodium thiosulfate solution (g/dm³)
50		40
	10	32
		24
	30	16
10	40	8

Task 14 Give the **independent** variable, **dependent** variable and two **control** variables for this experiment.

Independent variable:

Dependent variable:

Control variables:

Key Definitions
Independent variable
The variable you change.
Dependent variable
The variable you measure.
Control variable
A variable you keep the same.

DISCUSS — **X marks the spot... X marks the spot... X marks the spot...**

For each of the control variables you gave in Task 14, discuss why you think it's important that the variable is kept the same throughout the experiment. Can you think of any more control variables?

Practical 5: Rates of Reaction

Results and Analysis

Required Practical 5

Task 15 The table below shows some **example results** from the experiment. Calculate the **mean** time taken for the cross to disappear for the different concentrations. Give your answers to **the nearest second**.

Concentration of sodium thiosulfate solution (g/dm³)	Time taken for cross to disappear (seconds)			
	First trial	Second trial	Third trial	Mean
8	140	139	138	
16	74	76	74	
24	49	46	45	
32	40	37	36	
40	25	24	26	

Task 16 **Plot** the **concentration** of sodium thiosulfate solution against the **mean time** taken for the cross to disappear on the graph paper below. Draw a **line of best fit**.

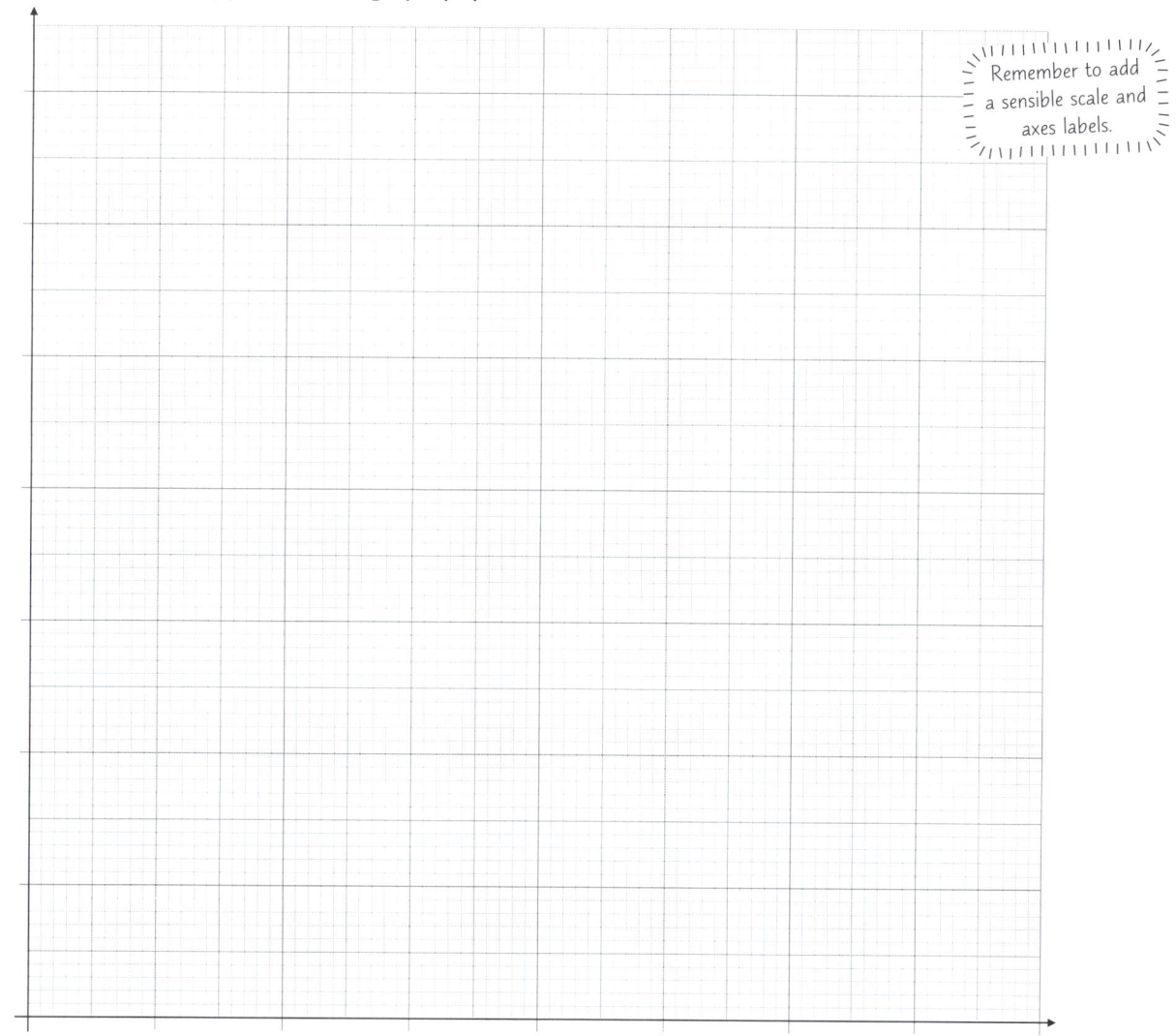

Remember to add a sensible scale and axes labels.

© CGP — not to be photocopied

Practical 5: Rates of Reaction

| Required Practical 5 | **Conclusions and Evaluation** |

Task 17 For each of the points below, **explain** why they are important for producing **accurate** and **reproducible** results.

Swirling the conical flask whilst adding the hydrochloric acid.

Printing out a black cross instead of drawing one.

Key Definitions
Accurate results
Results that are close to the true value.
Reproducible results
Results which are very similar when the experiment is repeated by someone else.

Task 18 You've now studied **two activities** investigating how **concentration** affects **rates of reactions**.

What does the graph you plotted in **Task 16** show you about the **relationship** between the independent and dependent variables in **Activity 2**?

....

....

Do your results from **Activity 2** line up with your results from **Activity 1**? Explain your answer.

....

....

Activity 1 involved **measuring gas production** using a measuring cylinder.
Activity 2 involved **timing** how long you could **see a black cross** through a solution.
Which of these methods of measurement is likely to be more **reproducible**? Explain your answer.

....

....

....

....

In **Activity 2**, the experiment was run **three times** and the **mean** time taken for the cross to disappear was calculated. Explain the impact this is likely to have had on the results.

....

....

Practical 5: Rates of Reaction © CGP — not to be photocopied

Exam-Style Questions

Required Practical 5

Task 19 Try these **exam-style** questions.

1   Marble chips are mostly made of calcium carbonate. They react with dilute hydrochloric acid to produce calcium chloride, carbon dioxide gas and water. The equation for this reaction is:

$$CaCO_{3(s)} + 2HCl_{(aq)} \rightarrow CaCl_{2(aq)} + CO_{2(g)} + H_2O_{(l)}$$

1.1 A student investigates the rate of this reaction at two different temperatures.
The graph below shows the volume of carbon dioxide produced over time at 20 °C.

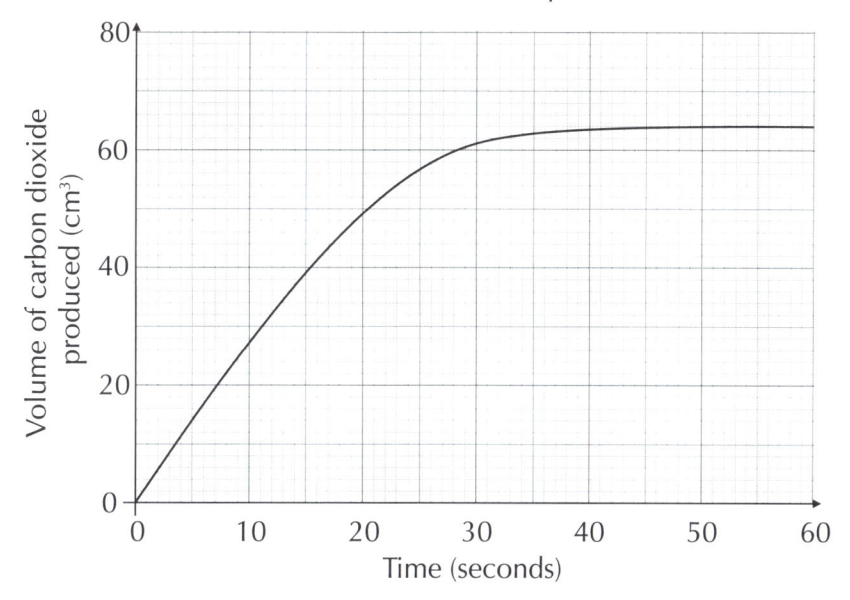

Sketch a curve on the graph for the results you would expect to see if the experiment was repeated at 25 °C.

[2]

1.2 Design an experiment to investigate the effect of surface area on the reaction between marble chips and hydrochloric acid.
Include details of the apparatus you would use and any measurements you would make.

....

....

....

....

....

....

....

....

....

[6]

[Total 8 marks]

© CGP — not to be photocopied

Practical 5: Rates of Reaction

Practical 6: Chromatography

Required Practical 6

Background Knowledge

This practical is all about **paper chromatography**. There's a good chance you've come across it before — it's a handy technique that can be used to **separate** and **identify** the different substances in a mixture.

Task 1 Fill in the gaps in the table below to complete the terms and their definitions.

Term	Definition
Soluble	
	Will not dissolve.
	The liquid that something is dissolved in.
Solute	
Solution	

Task 2 In chromatography there is always a **stationary phase** and a **mobile phase**. Label the stationary phase and the mobile phase on the chromatography experiment shown below.

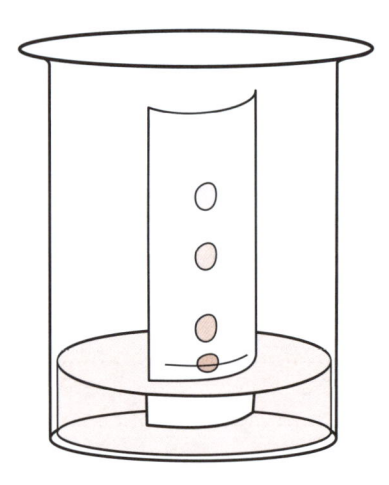

Key Definitions

Stationary Phase
In chromatography, a solid or really thick liquid where molecules are unable to move.

Mobile Phase
In chromatography, a gas or liquid where molecules are able to move.

Task 3 Explain, in terms of the stationary phase and mobile phase, why paper chromatography can be used to separate the substances in a mixture.

....
....
....
....

Practical

Required Practical 6

Task 4 Paper chromatography can be used to investigate the composition of a mixture of food colourings. The procedure for this experiment is shown below, but the steps have been mixed up. Put the steps in the correct order. The first one has been done for you.

1   D   **A** Mark how far up the paper the water travelled.

2   **B** Fill the bottom of the beaker to a depth of 1 cm with water, then place the bottom edge of the chromatography paper into the water.

3   **C** Wait until the water has nearly reached the top of the paper, then remove the paper from the beaker.

4   **D** Take a beaker and a piece of chromatography paper. Draw a line across the paper, approximately 2 cm from the bottom.

5   **E** Leave the paper to dry.

6   **F** At evenly spaced points along the line, place a spot of the unknown mixture and a spot of each of four known food colourings and label them.

Task 5 Look at step **D** in the method above. What would you use to draw the line, and why? Are there any other steps in the method where you might need to make similar considerations?

What you'd use

Why

Other steps

Task 6 Explain a modification you should make to the method shown above if the solvent is volatile.

....

....

Key Definition
Volatile
Has a low boiling point.

DISCUSS

I'm in my stationery phase — I just love a good gel pen...

Not all mixtures can be separated by paper chromatography, sadly. Discuss with a partner what needs to happen in order for it to work, and suggest some reasons why a mixture might not be separated by it.

© CGP — not to be photocopied

Practical 6: Chromatography

Required Practical 6

Results and Analysis

Task 7 Karim carried out the experiment using a mixture of food colourings, **M**, and known food colourings **W**, **X**, **Y** and **Z**. He obtained the chromatogram shown below.

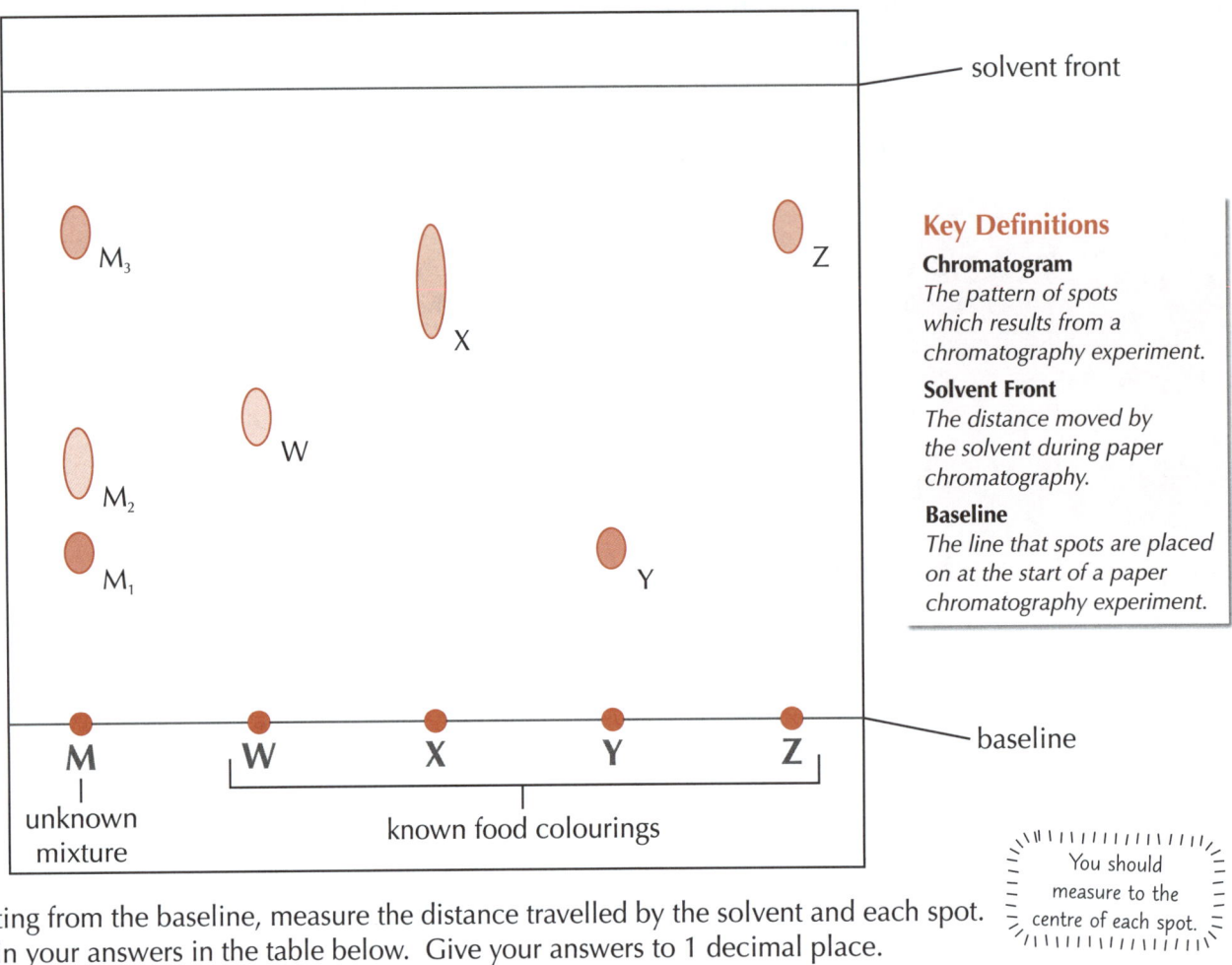

Key Definitions

Chromatogram
The pattern of spots which results from a chromatography experiment.

Solvent Front
The distance moved by the solvent during paper chromatography.

Baseline
The line that spots are placed on at the start of a paper chromatography experiment.

Starting from the baseline, measure the distance travelled by the solvent and each spot. Fill in your answers in the table below. Give your answers to 1 decimal place.

You should measure to the centre of each spot.

	Solvent	Spot M_1	Spot M_2	Spot M_3	Spot W	Spot X	Spot Y	Spot Z
Distance Travelled (cm)								

Task 8 An R_f value is a ratio that compares how far a substance travelled up a chromatogram compared to the solvent. It can be calculated using the equation:

$$R_f = \frac{\text{distance travelled by substance}}{\text{distance travelled by solvent}}$$

Use the equation to calculate the R_f value for each spot on the chromatogram. Give your answers to 2 significant figures.

	Spot M_1	Spot M_2	Spot M_3	Spot W	Spot X	Spot Y	Spot Z
R_f value							

Practical 6: Chromatography

Conclusions and Evaluation

Required Practical 6

Task 9 Which of food colourings **W**, **X**, **Y** or **Z**, could be present in mixture **M**? Tick the boxes of any you think are present.

W ☐   X ☐

Y ☐   Z ☐

Explain your choice(s)

Task 10 Karim looks closely at his chromatogram and notices that some of mixture **M** stayed on the baseline. Circle the correct options in the sentence below to give the **most accurate** conclusion he can draw about the **number of substances** in mixture **M**.

There are   **exactly / at least / fewer than**   **two / three / four**   substances in mixture **M**.

Suggest why some of the mixture stayed on the baseline.

....

Task 11 Explain two reasons why it would be a good idea for Karim to repeat the experiment using a **different solvent**.

1.

2.

Task 12 Karim wants to identify the substance that produced the spot M_2 on the chromatogram.

How could Karim modify his experiment to try and identify this substance?

....

....

DISCUSS

Out damned spot! Out! Oh wait, that's a chromatogram...

Why do you think it's important to remove the paper from the solvent before the solvent reaches the top of the paper? Discuss with a partner. (Hint: think about what you need to calculate R_f values.)

© CGP — not to be photocopied

Practical 6: Chromatography

Required Practical 6 — Exam-Style Questions

Task 13 Try these **exam-style** questions.

1 A student is doing a paper chromatography experiment to investigate the composition of a sample of ink, **S**. The student runs the sample against some known dyes, **L**, **M** and **N**, in water and in ethanol. **Figure 1** shows the chromatogram produced in water.

1.1 In **Figure 1**, the R_f value for dye **N** is 0.48.
The water moved 12.5 cm.
Using the formula for R_f, calculate the distance that dye **N** moved.

Figure 1

Chromatogram (water)

.... cm
[2]

1.2 Use **Figure 1** to explain which of dyes **L** and **N** will have the greater R_f value in water.

....
....
[1]

Table 1 shows the R_f values the student calculated for the same substances in ethanol.

Table 1

	S	L	M	N
R_f value(s) in ethanol	0.0, 0.27, 0.43, 0.73	0.21	0.43	1.1

1.3 The student's R_f value for dye **N** in **Table 1** is incorrect. How you can tell?

....
[1]

1.4 Use **Figure 1** and **Table 1** to explain which, if any, of dyes **L**, **M** and **N** could be in sample **S**.

....
....
....
[2]

1.5 Use **Table 1** to explain which of dyes **L** and **M** is more soluble in ethanol.

....
....
....
[3]

[Total 9 marks]

Practical 6: Chromatography

Practical 7: Identifying Ions

Background Knowledge

Required Practical 7

This practical is all about **testing**. Don't worry, you haven't opened an exam paper by mistake — I'm talking about using **chemical tests** (and a bit of detective work) to identify **mystery solutions**...

Task 1 Complete the sentences below by circling the **correct word** in each set of brackets.

Ionic compounds are made of positive and negative (atoms / **ions**) .

Metallic elements usually (gain / **lose**) electrons to form (**positive** / negative) ions.

Non-metals usually (**gain** / lose) electrons to form (positive / **negative**) ions.

(**Some** / All) ionic compounds dissolve in water to form solutions of their (**ions** / elements) .

Task 2 A solution was made by dissolving a single unidentified **ionic compound** in water. The solution was **tested** for various ions. The **results** of the tests are shown in the table.

Ion tested for	Ca^{2+}	Na^+	K^+	Fe^{2+}	CO_3^{2-}	Cl^-	Br^-	I^-
Ion present?	✗	✗	✓	✗	✗	✗	✓	✗

Name the ionic compound in this solution.

Task 3 Complete the equation below for the reaction between **sulfuric acid** and **sodium carbonate**.

Don't forget to include the state symbols.

$H_2SO_{4(aq)} + Na_2CO_{3(aq)} \rightarrow + CO_{2(g)} + $

Task 4 Complete the diagram below to show a method you could use to test if the **gas produced** in a reaction is **carbon dioxide**. Write down the **result** you would see if the test is **positive**.

If carbon dioxide is produced
....
....

DISCUSS — Carbonate — not the thing you open to get to the engine...

Discuss with a partner what you know about ionic compounds. What happens when an ionic compound dissolves in water? How are the properties of solid and dissolved ionic compounds different?

Required Practical 7

Practical

Task 5 A **flame test** is one way to test for certain **metal ions** in solutions. It uses the fact that some ions produce specific **colours** when heated in a flame. Below are **two different methods** for comparing different solutions using flame tests.

Procedure — using metal wire

1. Pour samples of the solutions to be tested into separate test tubes.
2. Light a Bunsen burner and set it to a blue flame.
3. Dip a nichrome or platinum wire into one of the samples.
4. Hold the wire with the tip in the Bunsen flame.
5. Observe and record the colour of the flame.
6. Clean the wire.
7. Repeat steps 3-6 for the rest of the samples, using the same wire.

Key Definition
Nichrome
An alloy of nickel and chromium. It has a high melting point and is not very reactive.

There are a couple of ways to clean the wire in a flame test — you can either dip it in dilute hydrochloric acid, then hold it in the Bunsen flame until it burns with no colour, or rub the end of the wire with emery paper (a kind of rough paper, a bit like sand paper).

Procedure — using wooden splints

1. Pour samples of the solutions to be tested into separate test tubes.
2. Light a Bunsen burner and set it to a blue flame.
3. Soak one end of a wooden splint in one of the samples.
4. Hold the damp part of the splint in the edge of the Bunsen flame.
5. Observe and record the colour of the flame around the splint.
6. Remove the splint from the flame before it catches fire.
7. Repeat steps 3-6 for the rest of the samples, using a new splint each time.

Suggest **two advantages** and **two disadvantages** of using wooden splints instead of metal wire to carry out this type of test in a school lab.

Advantages of using wooden splints	Disadvantages of using wooden splints

Practical 7: Identifying Ions

Practical

Required Practical 7

Task 6 This task is about a test that can be used to identify **carbonate ions** in solution. The **equipment** used in the test is shown below.

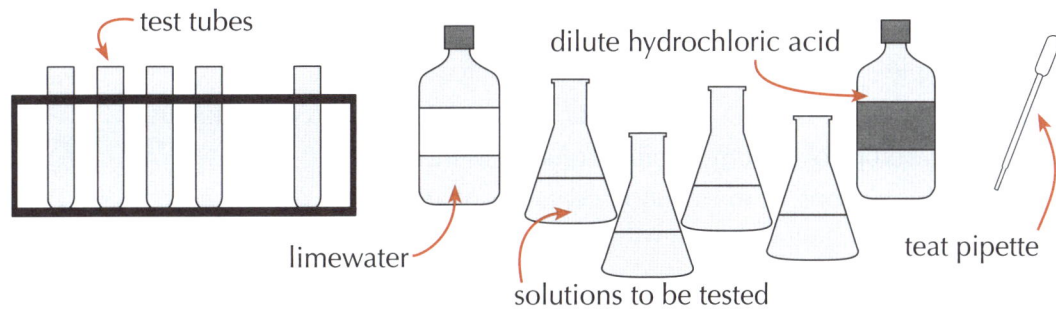

This test is based on the way **carbonates** react with **acids**. Describe in words what you would **observe** when an acid reacts with a metal carbonate in solution, and why.

....

....

....

Procedure

1. Pour limewater into one of the test tubes until it is about one-quarter full. Put samples of each of the solutions you want to test into separate test tubes.
2. Add a few drops of hydrochloric acid to the first sample solution.
3. Watch to see if any bubbles are given off. If there are no bubbles, move on to the next sample.
4. If you do see bubbles, use a teat pipette to collect some of the gas that is produced.
5. Put the tip of the pipette into the limewater and release the collected gas. Repeat the process of collecting and releasing the gas several times and observe any changes in the limewater.
6. Replace the limewater, then move on to the next sample.
7. Carry on until all the samples have been tested, recording your observations as you go.

Explain how **step 5** of this procedure will tell you if the solution being tested contains **carbonate ions**.

....

....

For each sample where a gas is produced, why do you think that the process of collecting the gas given off and bubbling it through limewater is done **several times**?

....

....

....

Required Practical 7

Practical

Task 7 The procedure below can be used to test for the presence of **sulfate ions** in a solution.

Procedure

1. Pour out a sample of the solution you want to test into a test tube.
2. Use a dropping pipette to add a few drops of hydrochloric acid to your sample.
3. Next, add a few drops of barium chloride solution to the test tube.
4. Record your observations. If the solution contains sulfate ions, a white precipitate of barium sulfate will form.

Key Definition
Precipitate
A solid product of a reaction that forms in a solution.

Acid is added to the sample at the start of this test.
Why is **hydrochloric acid** used instead of **sulfuric acid**?

....
....
....

You don't need to know it for GCSE, but if you're wondering: you add acid at the start in case the sample contains carbonate ions. Carbonate ions react with barium chloride in a similar way to sulfate ions, but they also react with acids, so adding the acid gets them out of the way before you do the sulfate test.

Task 8 A test that can be used to identify three different **halide ions** is described below.

Procedure

1. Pour out a sample of the solution you want to test into a test tube.
2. Use a dropping pipette to add a few drops of nitric acid to your sample.
3. Next, add a few drops of silver nitrate solution to the test tube.
4. Record your observations. If the solution contains chloride, bromide or iodide ions, a precipitate will form.

   Chloride ions form a white precipitate of silver chloride, bromide ions produce cream-coloured silver bromide, and iodide ions form pale yellow silver iodide.

Key Definition
Halide ion
A 1– ion of a halogen element.

This test works best if samples of **known** chloride, bromide and iodide solutions are tested first, before any **unknown** solutions. Suggest why it's particularly useful to test **reference samples** first in this test.

....
....
....

DISCUSS

More tests here than you can shake a wooden splint at...

You've got the information about lots of individual tests here. Discuss how you would combine them to do tests on several unknown solutions. What's the most efficient way to identify a series of mystery salts?

Practical 7: Identifying Ions

Conclusions and Evaluation

Required Practical 7

Task 9 A student carried out **flame tests** and the tests for **carbonates**, **sulfates** and **halides** on a series of solutions of known compounds. Their results are shown below.

Solution	lithium chloride	sodium chloride	potassium chloride	calcium chloride	copper chloride
Cation	lithium Li^+	sodium Na^+	potassium K^+	calcium Ca^{2+}	copper Cu^{2+}
Flame colour	crimson	yellow	lilac	orange-red	green

Solution	sodium carbonate	sodium sulfate	sodium chloride	sodium bromide	sodium iodide
Anion	carbonate CO_3^{2-}	sulfate SO_4^{2-}	chloride Cl^-	bromide Br^-	iodide I^-
Result in carbonate test	limewater turns cloudy	no change	no change	no change	no change
Result in sulfate test	no change	white precipitate	no change	no change	no change
Result in halide test	no change	no change	white precipitate	cream precipitate	yellow precipitate

The student then tested samples of three **unknown solutions**, **A**, **B** and **C**.
Each solution contained a different **ionic compound**, composed of ions given in the tables above.
The results of these tests are shown below.

Solution	Flame test	Carbonate test	Sulfate test	Halide test
A	orange-red	no change	no change	cream precipitate
B	crimson	limewater turns cloudy	no change	no change
C	yellow	no change	no change	yellow precipitate

Using the information in the tables above, suggest which **ionic compounds** have been dissolved to make solutions **A**, **B** and **C**.

A is .... solution.

B is .... solution.

C is .... solution.

| Required Practical 7 | **Conclusions and Evaluation** |

Task 10
Michelle carries out **flame tests** on samples of three solutions, **X**, **Y** and **Z**, using a loop of nichrome wire in a Bunsen burner flame. Michelle knows that one of the solutions is **lithium sulfate**, one is **sodium sulfate** and one is **potassium sulfate**, but she doesn't know which one is which. Her observations are shown in the table below.

Solution	Observation in flame test
X	lilac flame
Y	yellow flame
Z	yellow flame

Michelle made a **mistake** while she was carrying out her experiment.
Using the table, explain what you think her mistake was.

....
....
....

Task 11
The procedure for an **additional test** for **cations** is given below.

Procedure
1. Pour samples of the solutions to be tested into separate test tubes.
2. Add a few drops of sodium hydroxide solution to each test tube.
3. Record any observations. Some cations form white or coloured metal hydroxide precipitates when they react with hydroxide ions.
4. If a precipitate forms, add more sodium hydroxide solution to test whether the precipitate redissolves with excess sodium hydroxide. Record any observations.

Key Definitions
Cation
A positive ion.
Anion
A negative ion.

Think about why carrying out this **additional test** for cations, alongside flame tests, might be useful. Explain your thoughts below.

DISCUSS — **Another chemystery solved — it's elementary...**
A lot of these tests work best if there's just one salt in the solution you're testing. For each test, discuss with a partner what might happen if more than one salt was present. Could you get any useful results?

Practical 7: Identifying Ions © CGP — not to be photocopied

Exam-Style Questions

Required Practical 7

Task 12 Try these **exam-style questions**.

1   A student carried out tests to investigate the ions present in a series of known solutions.
    The student tested a sample of each solution by adding sodium hydroxide solution.
    Many metal cations react with hydroxide ions to form precipitates.

    The student's observations are shown in the table below.

Solution	Observation
iron(II) chloride, $FeCl_2$	green precipitate
iron(III) chloride, $FeCl_3$	brown precipitate
aluminium chloride, $AlCl_3$	white precipitate, redissolves with excess NaOH
copper(II) chloride, $CuCl_2$	blue precipitate
calcium chloride, $CaCl_2$	white precipitate
magnesium chloride, $MgCl_2$	white precipitate

1.1 Write the ionic equation, including state symbols, for the formation of
    the green precipitate of iron(II) hydroxide in this test.

    ....

    [2]

    The student carries out the same test on a solution of another, unknown salt.
    It forms a white precipitate which does not redissolve with excess sodium hydroxide solution.

1.2 The student believes this solution contains calcium ions.
    Describe a test the student could carry out that would confirm this.
    Include the result you would expect if the cations in the salt are calcium ions.

    ....

    ....

    ....

    ....

    [3]

1.3 The student believes that the anions in the unknown salt are bromide ions.
    Describe a test the student could carry out to confirm this.
    Include the result the student should expect to see and the ionic equation, including state
    symbols, for the reaction that will take place if the anions are bromide ions.

    ....

    ....

    ....

    ....

    ....

    [4]

    [9 marks]

Practical 7: Identifying Ions

Practical 8: Water Purification

Required Practical 8

Background Knowledge

Water purification might not be the most glamorous subject, but it's pretty useful. Without **clean water**, we'd all be drinking nothing but fruit juice and bathing in milk like Cleopatra.

Task 1 **Litmus** and **universal indicator** are two examples of indicators. Fill in the table below **comparing** these two indicators. Give as much information as you can.

> **Key Definition**
> **Indicator**
> *A dye that changes colour depending on the pH.*

	Litmus	Universal Indicator
Description of colour change		
What would you use it for?		
How is it used? E.g. solution, paper or both		

Task 2 Water from different **natural sources** can be treated to supply **potable water**. The main sources are **fresh water** and **sea water**. Complete the mind map below to **compare** these two sources of potable water.

> **Key Definition**
> **Potable water**
> *Water that is safe for humans to drink.*

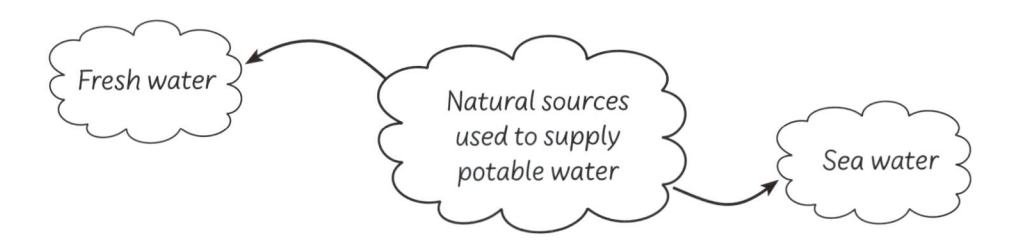

Fresh water ← Natural sources used to supply potable water → Sea water

Think about why each type of water needs treating, how it's treated and where the different supplies are used.

Indicators are just dyeing to tell you what the pH is...

DISCUSS With a partner, see if you can remember any other indicators you've used. How do they compare to litmus and universal indicator? What other ways are there to investigate the pH of a solution?

Practical — Activity 1

Required Practical 8

Task 3 In the box below, give a brief **outline** of how you could use the equipment shown to determine the **pH** of a series of **water samples**.

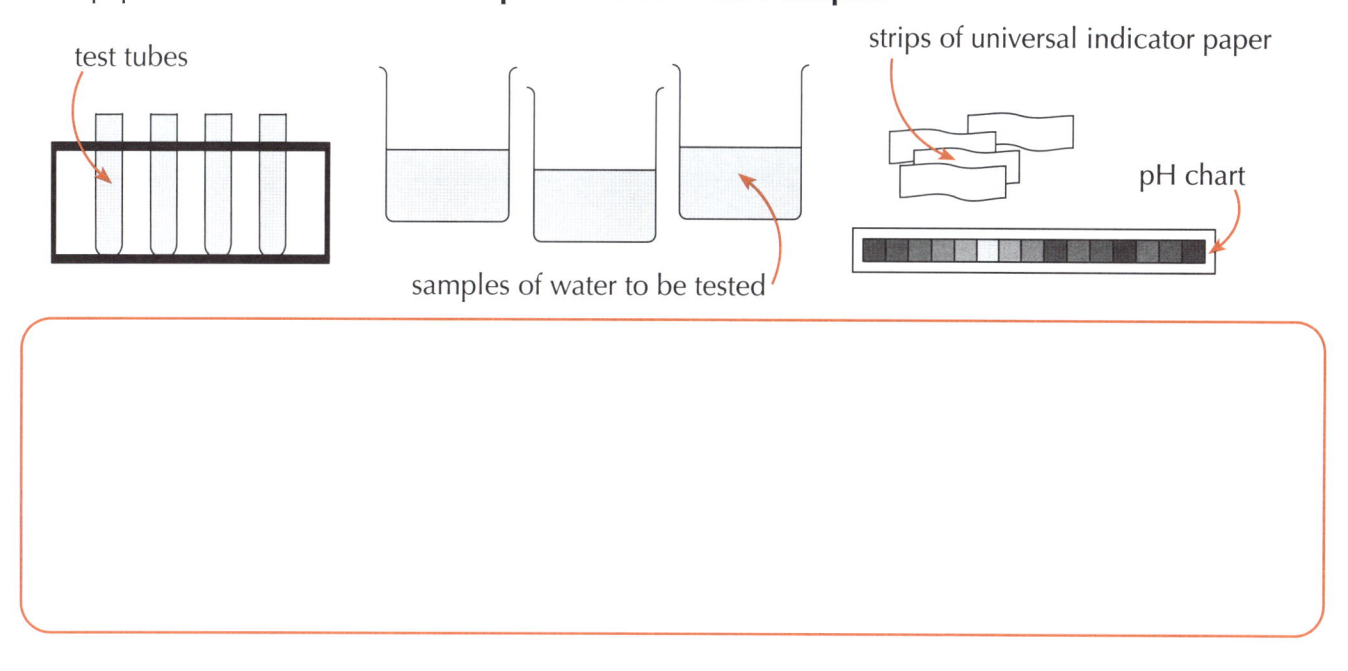

- test tubes
- samples of water to be tested
- strips of universal indicator paper
- pH chart

Task 4 This procedure can be used to find the mass of **dissolved solids** in a sample of water.

Procedure

1. Use a mass balance to accurately measure the mass of an evaporating basin. Record the mass of the empty basin.
2. Place the evaporating basin on a tripod and gauze over a Bunsen burner.
3. Pour a measured volume of the water sample into the basin.
4. Light the Bunsen burner and heat the evaporating basin until most of the water has evaporated.
5. Allow the basin to cool and the remaining water to evaporate. Crystals of any dissolved solids should be left behind in the basin.
6. Re-weigh the basin on the mass balance. Record the mass of the basin and its contents.

The **mass balance** used in this experiment should be able to measure a mass in grams to at least **two decimal places**. Suggest why this is important.

....

....

Sometimes, this method will give a value for the mass of dissolved solids that is **lower** than the **true mass**. Suggest one reason this might happen.

....

....

Practical 8: Water Purification

Required Practical 8: Analysis and Evaluation

Task 5 Give one **disadvantage** of using **universal indicator** to measure the pH of a water sample. Suggest what you could use **instead** that would address this disadvantage.

....
....
....

Task 6 Miles tested the **pH** of water samples from three **different sources**. His results are shown in the table.

Sample	A	B	C
pH	7	6	4

Miles wrote down two **conclusions**.
For each one, explain why Miles was **wrong** to make that conclusion from his results.

Sample A is neutral, so it must be pure water with no dissolved substances.

....
....

Sample C is more acidic than sample B, so C must have a greater mass of dissolved substances than B.

....
....

Task 7 Miles used **evaporation** to find the mass of dissolved solid in a 10 cm³ sample of water from **source C**. His results are shown in the table.

Evaporation of 10 cm³ sample from source C	
Mass of empty evaporating basin	22.46 g
Mass of basin after evaporating water sample	22.74 g

Calculate the **concentration** of dissolved solid in the water sample from source C in **g/dm³**.

DISCUSS — Water source C is not necessarily "water, source: sea"
You can't tell from these tests what substances are dissolved in a water sample.
Discuss with a partner what sort of tests might help to identify the dissolved substances.

Practical 8: Water Purification

Practical — Activity 2

Required Practical 8

Task 8 The apparatus shown in the diagram below can be used to **distil** a sample of water. Use the diagram to **complete the steps** of the procedure.

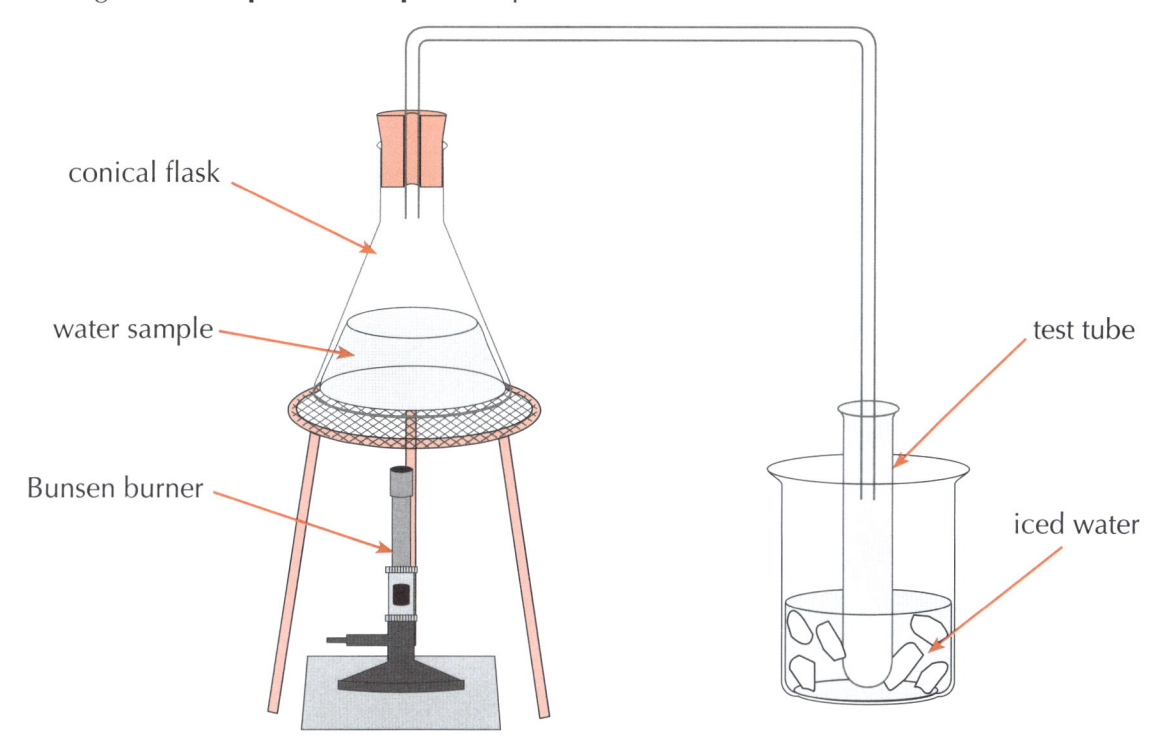

Procedure

1. Stand an empty test tube _____ .

2. Put _____ in a conical flask, and place this on a tripod and gauze over a Bunsen burner.

3. Connect the conical flask to _____ via glass or rubber tubing which passes through _____ .

4. Light the Bunsen burner and _____ .

   The steam will pass through the tubing and condense _____ .

5. Continue gently _____ until you have 1-2 cm of water in the test tube.

6. Turn off the Bunsen burner. You will have _____ in the test tube.

   Any _____ or insoluble impurities from the original water sample will _____ .

DISCUSS

Yes, those are supposed to be bits of ice, not crisps...

The diagram above shows only the essential equipment to carry out the experiment. What other pieces of equipment might be useful to make this experiment go smoothly? Discuss with a partner.

Required Practical 8

Practical — Activity 2

Task 9 Instead of using the set-up shown in **Task 8**, you can also separate water from dissolved solids by simple distillation using a **condenser**. Draw and label a **diagram** showing the set-up for this method.

Include labels to show where the water goes in and out of the condenser.

Task 10 Water containing dissolved substances is a **mixture**. Explain how you could use the different properties of pure substances and mixtures to **confirm** that the product of a distillation experiment is **pure water**.

Key Definitions

Mixture
Two or more substances that are combined, but not chemically bonded.

Pure substance
A substance containing only one element or compound.

Practical 8: Water Purification © CGP — not to be photocopied

Results, Analysis and Evaluation

Required Practical 8

Task 11 **Evaporation** and **distillation** can both be used to separate dissolved solids from liquids. Suggest why distillation has been used instead of evaporation in this part of this practical.

....
....
....

Task 12 A student is given instructions for the procedure shown in **Task 8**. The instructions contain the following **warnings**. For each one, say why you think it would cause a problem if the advice is not followed.

Hint: Both these warnings are to stop the water ending up in the wrong place. What would happen if it did?

| When heating the conical flask, do not allow the water to boil too vigorously and reach the top of the flask. | Make sure the end of the tube leading into the test tube always remains well above the level of the distilled water that has been collected. |

Task 13 Look back at **Task 6** and **Task 7**. Miles continued his investigation of his water samples. He distilled a sample of water from source C. He then **repeated** his tests from Tasks 6 and 7 on samples of the distilled water he collected. Explain how this will help Miles **confirm** that he carried out the distillation correctly, and what **results** he should expect.

....
....
....

DISCUSS

De-still-ation is how they make sparkling water...
Compare the distillation apparatus used in Task 8 with the diagram you drew in Task 9. Discuss with a partner the advantages and disadvantages of each method. Which would you use, and why?

© CGP — not to be photocopied

Practical 8: Water Purification

Required Practical 8

Exam-Style Questions

Task 14 Try these **exam-style** questions.

1 A student is investigating the water quality of a local river. The student collects a number of water samples from a part of the river near their home over the course of one afternoon.

1.1 Suggest two ways the student could improve this sampling to be more representative.

1 ....

....

2 ....

....

[2]

1.2 The student tests a sample of pure water alongside the samples from the river. Suggest why the student does this.

....

....

....

[1]

1.3 The student discovers that their supply of pure water has been contaminated with an impurity. The student believes that this impurity is sodium chloride. Describe how the student could:
- obtain a solid sample of the dissolved impurity,
- measure the mass of the sample of the impurity obtained, and
- carry out tests to confirm the water contains sodium chloride.

....

....

....

....

....

....

....

....

....

....

....

[6]

[Total 9 marks]

Practical 8: Water Purification